Havanese

◇

By Zoila Portuondo Guerra
Translated by Jane McManus

i·5
PRESS

Photos by Herbert R. Axelrod, Norvia Behling, Sandra Block, Carolina Biological Supply, Doskocil, Isabelle Français, Tony George, Zoila Potuondo Guerra, James Hayden-Yoav, James R. Hayden, RBP, Dwight R. Kuhn, Dr. Dennis Kunkel, Mikki Pet Products, Phototake, Jean Claude Revy, Nikki Sussman, Alice van Kempen, Theo von Sambeek and C. James Webb.
Illustrations by Renée Low.

Original Print ISBN: 978-1-59378-217-7

i-5 Publishing, LLC™
3 Burroughs, Irvine, CA 92618
www.facebook.com/i5press
www.i5publishing.com

My Havanese

PUT YOUR PUPPY'S FIRST PICTURE HERE

Dog's Name _____

Date _____ Photographer _____

Ears: Of medium length; the leather, when extended, reaches halfway to the nose. They are set high on the skull, slightly above the endpoint of the zygomatic arch, and are broad at the base, showing a distinct fold.

Neck: Of moderate length, in balance with the height and length of the dog. It carries a slight arch and blends smoothly into the shoulders.

Eyes: Dark brown, large, almond-shaped, and set rather widely apart. Dark eyes are preferred irrespective of coat color.

Nose: Broad and squarish, fitting a full and rectangular muzzle, with no indication of snipiness. The pigment on the nose and lips is complete, solid black for all colors except for the chocolate dog which has complete solid, dark chocolate brown pigment.

Chest: Deep, rather broad in front, and reaches the elbow. The ribs are well sprung. There is a moderate tuck-up.

Forequarters: Shoulder layback is moderate, lying not more than 40 degrees off vertical. The upper arm is relatively short, but there is sufficient angle between the shoulder and upper arm to set the legs well under the body with a pronounced forechest. The elbows turn neither in nor out, and are tight to the body. Forelegs are well-boned and straight when viewed from any angle. The distance from the foot to the elbow is equal to the distance from elbow to withers. The pasterns are short, strong and flexible, very slightly sloping.

Physical Characteristics of the Havanese

(from the American Kennel Club breed standard)

Topline: Straight but not level, rising slightly from withers to rump.

Tail: High-set and plumed with long, silky hair. It arcs forward over the back, but neither lies flat on the back nor is tightly curled.

Body: Measured from point of shoulder to point of buttocks, is slightly longer than the height at the withers. This length comes from the rib cage and not from the short, well-muscled loin.

Hindquarters: The hind legs are well-boned and muscular through the thigh, with moderate angulation. The hocks are short and turn neither in nor out. The hind feet fall slightly behind a perpendicular line from point of buttock when viewed from the side. Hind feet have well arched toes and turn neither in nor out.

Coat: The coat is double, but without the harsh standoff guard hair and woolly undercoat usually associated with double coats. Rather, it is soft and light in texture throughout, though the outer coat carries slightly more weight. The long hair is abundant and, ideally, wavy.

Color: All colors are acceptable, singly or in any combination.

Feet: Round, with well arched toes, and turning neither in nor out.

Contents

A "fleecy" wonder from Havana, the Havanese belongs to the Bichon family that dates back to ancient times.

HISTORY OF THE
HAVANESE

THE BICHON BREEDS

Before you read the particular history of the Havanese, you should know that this breed belongs to the family of dogs called Bichons, who were known throughout Europe for many centuries. The French word *Bichon* means "fleecy dog" and is thought to be a contraction of the word *Barbichon*, or "bearded." It is probably related to the French word *Barbet*, which also refers to an ancient breed of water spaniel similar to the Poodle, from which all Bichons of the world are descended.

With time and use, the term *Bichon* has become synonymous with a dog completely covered with hair, with a delightful people-oriented personality. In cynology circles, the term *Bichon* is applied to a group of dog breeds whose distant ancestors are the same. Bichon-type dogs have a long ancestry. References indicate that they were known in ancient Greece. Some centuries later, they appeared in all countries of the Mediterranean Basin and became very fashionable in Europe during the Renaissance. In the 15th and 16th centuries, they were introduced to other parts of the world through the expansion of the Spanish Empire that dominated Middle Europe at that time. The Spanish used their maritime power to conquer and colonize much of the New World, as well as some parts of Asia and Africa. It was said of Charles V,

"Portrait of a Young Woman," painted by Vicente Escobar, shows a young lady with a Blanquito de la Habana. Escobar was a famous Cuban portrait painter (1757-1854), and this is the earliest (and only) painting of this extinct breed. The original is in the archives of the Salas del Museo Nacional de Cuba in Havana, where it has not been on exhibit for many years.

Hapsburg Holy Roman Emperor and King of Spain, that he presided over an empire so vast the sun never set on it.

Thanks to this dispersion of Bichons over many parts of the world during the 16th century, we came to have a number of perfectly developed and defined breeds. In some of these countries, Bichons were mixed with other similar-type breeds and the outcome was different, distinct breeds with new images all their own. Different cultures and tastes produced different dogs, such as the following breeds.

MALTESE

This breed's long white coat hangs evenly down each side of the body, and it measures no more than 10 inches tall at the withers. This breed was described in 200 BC under the Latin name *Canis Melitaeus*, which could have referred to the island of Malta or the Sicilian town of Melita, and was concentrated in Italy. The Maltese is the tiniest of the Bichons and weighs less than 7 pounds, usually 4 to 6 pounds.

BICHON FRISE

Exclusively white and somewhat larger than the Maltese, its coat is *frisé* or curly, and shaped to the body. It is traced to the Bichon Tenerife of the Canary Islands but was developed in Belgium and France. Like the Maltese, the Bichon Frise has many admirers

This pet Havanese, named Fama, was photographed in Cuba. Although not as glamorous as many of the show dogs, the pet Havaneses have terrific, loving personalities.

The Maltese is counted among the world's most glorious and glamorous breeds. Its silky floor-length coat drapes luxuriously over its 4- to 6-pound body. This is an American champion Maltese.

As puppies, the Bichon breeds are astoundingly similar. This snow-white trio is Maltese. Notice that the dark pigmentation on the eye rims and noses is present in puppyhood.

Unlike the Havanese, which is presented in the show ring in its "natural" coat, the Maltese is presented with its full-length coat groomed to perfection.

all over the world, not just in its native land. The breed is medium sized, classified in the FCI's Group 9 (Companion and Toy dogs) and the AKC's Non-Sporting Group. The breed stands 9 to 12 inches high.

BOLOGNESE

Somewhat more square in shape than the other Bichons, the Bolognese has a flocked coat and

Italy's Bichon breed, the Bolognese resembles its Bichon relatives with its pure white coat, dark eyes and black nose.

The snow white powderpuff we call the Bichon Frise possesses a prominent head, slightly rounded, with "halos" around its eyes. Of all the Bichon breeds, this dog has the most distinctive head.

The Bichon Frise is another Bichon breed that derived from dogs indigenous to an island; in this case, the Canary Islands.

is named for the area where it first made its mark, Bologna, Italy. Like the Maltese and Bichon Frise, the Bolognese is a solid white dog without markings of any kind. The breed stands 10 to 12 inches high.

LÖWCHEN

The Löwchen is a small, square dog of varied colors with a straight coat that is clipped to give it the appearance of a lion, thus giving the breed the name "Little Lion Dog." It was known in Germany, France and Spain in the 16th century and is now considered a rare breed, although it has attracted attention on both sides of the Atlantic. Like the Havanese, the Löwchen can come in many colors, not just the traditional white. In size, the Löwchen can stand 10 to 13 inches and weigh 8 to 18 pounds.

COTON DE TULÉAR

The little-known Bichon of Madagascar derived from the same Bichon stock that arrived on the island of Tenerife, whence came the Bichon Frise. In French, *coton* means "cotton" and this describes the breed's desired coat type. The Coton de Tuléar was recognized by the Fédération Cynologique Internationale (FCI) in 1970, though the breed had been a favorite of French nobles in the 17th century. The breed stands 10 to 12 inches high. In

Cotton is this Bichon's calling card. The Coton de Tuléar originated in Madagascar but is considered a French breed.

The Löwchen is a Bichon that is clipped to resemble a lion.

Bred from similar stock as the well-known Poodle, which figures prominently in the Havanese's development, the Portuguese Water Dog shares many of the same characteristics, including a waterproof coat.

ships and crews from all parts of the world, including those bringing Spanish products, people and customs. All of them were welcomed by the warmth of Havana.

The Havanese adorned and enlivened the homes of aristocratic Cubans during the 18th and 19th centuries. At the turn of the 20th century, due to changes in fashion, taste, interests and influences, the Havanese was dismissed from the mansion but readily accepted in more modest homes.

To understand how all this happened, however, we have to take a closer look at history. When the Spaniards came to Cuba, they brought certain dogs that were useful to them in the colonization process: Mastiffs, Spanish Bloodhounds

color, the breed is mainly white, though it can have champagne markings on the head and body. Some examples are seen in black and white.

DEVELOPMENT OF THE HAVANESE

The Havanese originated in Cuba from an earlier breed known as Blanquito de la Habana. This white dog with a "geographic" last name undoubtedly came from the famous port that was visited over the centuries by

The Havanese on Cuba's largest tobacco plantation, owned by the world-famous Alejandro Robaina, the only living person after whom a cigar is named. The Robaina Vega dates back to 1845 in Havana. Here Dr. Herbert Axelrod visits with Sr. Robaina and his Havanese.

(FACING PAGE:) As young puppies, the Bichon breeds all appear adorable and furry! These two pups are Coton de Tuléar.

A Cuban postage stamp celebrating the nation's only extant purebred dog: the Havanese.

and Greyhounds. They were big, strong dogs that could hunt, protect property and, when necessary, fight. These weren't the only dogs in Spain, however, and once the epoch of conquest gave way to a more stabilized colonial life, the Spaniards began to bring to the island smaller companion dogs to be enjoyed in the intimate life of the family.

Bichons had become fashionable lapdogs in Europe during the Renaissance, perhaps a little earlier. They were "very small...very charming and alert...with hair so soft it seems like silk...bred by dames and nobles for their entertainment because of the tricks and games they were capable of learning and performing." This description occurs in Victor Manuel Patiño's *Plantas Cultivadas y Animales Domésticos en la América Equinoccial.*

What better distraction on an island like Cuba, which was extremely isolated from Spain during the first two centuries of colonization! The voyage sometimes could take as long as six months. The Cubans, of course, were anxious to keep abreast of the most refined European customs. In those days, Spain maintained a fierce commercial monopoly over Cuba, and it is probable that the first lapdogs to reach the island came directly from Spain or, via Spain, from other lands that had contact with the country.

Because of this monopoly, as well as the efforts of other European powers to grab the wealth of the Americas, Cuba carried on what has been termed a "ransom trade" with French, English and Dutch pirates. Through these trades, both sides—pirates and colonists— acquired much of what they couldn't otherwise get in legal trade. It is not impossible that these contacts introduced some lapdogs into Cuba, especially at the end of the 17th century.

All this leads to the conclusion that the most remote origins of the Havanese go back to the Spanish water dogs and Bichon-type lapdogs, although other Hispanic dogs of similar type may also have played a role. The Bichon brought from Europe to Cuba adapted to the island's particular diet and climate and to the customs and tastes of the residents. Eventually, these conditions gave birth to a different dog, smaller than its predecessors, with a completely white coat of a silkier texture closer to the preferences and luxurious living conditions of its new breeders. This dog was the Blanquito de la Habana.

Many writers point to the early 18th century as the period when a dog that the British called "White Cuban" was recognized in

For years, the Havanese has been confused with the original Cuban Bichon breed, the now-extinct Blanquito de la Habana. Today's Havanese should not be referred to as a "Havanese Silk Dog." This is the author with a bitch called Esmeralda de la Giraldilla, a Cuban champion.

England with some fanfare. This Blanquito de la Habana or Perro de Seda de la Habana (Havanese Silk Dog), as it was later called, has erroneously been identified as the Havanese or the Maltese, and this has led to confusions and misconceptions.

Although little was printed in Cuba in that period, by the end of the 18th century, we find clear evidence that the Blanquito de la Habana had multiplied in the wealthy homes of Havana. One such testimony is that of the famous Countess of Merlin, a

Cuban-born resident in France, in her *Viaje a la Habana* (Trip to Havana). She describes the typical gifts she received from her Cuban family before returning to France: "...two little dogs about six inches long, with large round black eyes that shine through long hair as white as snow, lie in baskets adorned with rose-colored ribbons awaiting the departure..." It is curious that this Cuban residing in France, who traveled in the most refined society of Paris and Madrid and must have had contact with European lapdogs, should consider the Blanquito de la Habana so unusual and typical of her native isle that she never compared it to any other breed.

Other evidence appears in "Portrait of a Young Woman," painted in 1797 by Cuba's first important painter, Vicente Escobar, whose subjects were upper-class Cubans. It shows an aristocratic young woman holding a Blanquito de la Habana in her arms. At the end of the 18th century, the *Papel Periódico de la Habana*, the island's most important daily newspaper, carried notices of lost dogs and advertisements for "fine dogs." ("Fine dog" was synonymous with Maltese, the name that Cubans popularly and incorrectly applied to the Havanese, and still do.) In addition, a critical journal of 1800, *El Regañon de la Habana*, attacked the fashionable customs of the wealthy, such as the hours spent bathing and grooming their lapdogs.

The 18th century marked the beginning of the consolidation of Cuban tastes and styles, although much of the Cuban landed gentry zealously followed refined European customs, imitating the latest fashions with surprising success. It was said that, in Havana, the upper classes dressed and lived like those in Madrid, London or Paris, and that Havana featured performances by the most famous European theater and opera companies (for the rich, naturally). At the same time, living conditions on the island, the climate—so different from that of the Continent—as well as other factors had formed a Cuban character that was different from

The famed Blanquito de la Habana derived from the original Spanish Bichon-type dogs and was the basis for the Havanese, a breed known for the silken texture of its coat.

the peninsular character. Naturally, these cultural changes also affected dogs.

The Blanquito de la Habana was, like any other dog breed, a clear product of the taste and culture of its breeders, who imposed the seal of their period and circumstances. They preferred a miniature white dog, with long, silky hair and an extremely loving and lively character. The *Diccionario Enciclopédico Hispanoamericano*, published in 1894, described it as follows: "the little Havanese dog, *Canis vellerosus*, exists in Havana; it is smaller [than the Maltese] and is covered with a type of fleece that is long, curly, white and satiny or silky. The specimens taken to Europe have been unable to resist the change of climate for very long."

Finally, listen to the description of the Blanquito given by the Spanish writer Alejandro Bon in *El Perro*: "It is a veritable snowball, or to put it better, a ball of white silk, with a black nose and lively, bright eyes almost hidden behind the long hair that hangs from its head. It is very small and weighs no more than 2.5 kilograms. Since its long hair falls to the ground, its feet are invisible and it seems to advance by dragging them. Its tail is like a plume, very fluffy, inclined over the back and to one side. It has a lively, intelligent character and,

As more and more European traditions were adopted in Cuba in the 19th century, the Cubans became enamored with the German and French Poodles, which were crossed with the existing Blanquito to create today's Havanese. Esmeralda de la Giraldilla, owned by Merita Batista and Annia Barroso.

although it is very loyal to its masters, it can be somewhat disdainful on occasion. This dog requires constant bathing and special care in order to keep it healthy."

J. Brouwer Etchecopar, a pioneer of cynological studies in Cuba, wrote the following in *Razas Caninas*: "There is considerable confusion concerning the Blanquito Cubano. According to Lloyd, it is a cross between a German or French Toy Poodle and a Maltese, but larger than the

(FACING PAGE) The Poodle has been involved in the development of more breeds than any other dog. No wonder! Considered the height of fashion, elegance and athleticism, the Poodle contributed its intelligence, non-shedding coat and people-loving personality.

latter and with hair that touches the ground. The name Maltese is also somewhat confusing, for that is what this dog is called in the capital of Cuba, whereas in other European countries it is known as either Havanese or Blanquito de la Habana, and we haven't yet been able to unravel these anomalies." The only problem here is that Lloyd and Etchecopar are no longer talking about the Blanquito de la Habana, but rather the Bichon Havanese; although the two breeds belong to the Bichon family, their characteristics are notably different.

When Spain ended the trade monopoly in Cuba, the island began to enjoy the advantages that its privileged geographic position presented. Immigrants

arrived on the island to work the fertile land and establish their businesses. The French are a case in point, particularly those who had lived in the French colonies of Santo Domingo and Haiti. When revolution erupted there, thousands of French settlers immigrated to Cuba, bringing not only their wealth but also their culture and their lifestyle, which naturally included their dogs.

Caniches or Poodles, likely originally from Germany but adopted by France, became known in 19th-century Cuba. Some may have arrived with the French immigrants, but their predecessors could also have come from Germany, via France, or from Spain itself, since these countries had a direct relationship with the breed.

With the arrival in Cuba of a greater number of Poodles, the Blanquito de la Habana began its transformation. It is not surprising that the Criollo landowners were somewhat bowled over by these new dogs and considered it advantageous to cross them with their native breed, perhaps with the idea of increasing the size and varying the color of the Blanquito de la Habana. Thus, gradually, a new breed arrived on the scene: the Havanese.

The Havanese, then, originated in the 19th century as the result of mating Blanquitos de la Habana with Poodles. In this

The Poodle contributed much to the Havanese's development, but the breed more closely resembles its ancestor, the Blanquito de la Habana.

mating, it is evident that the type of the Bichon remain unaltered. In reality, the Cuban Poodle breeder has had to make every effort to eliminate from his lines the elongated body and short legs of the that were definitively imposed in these early crosses, not only through genetics but through the traditionally cultivated taste that gave preference to this breed's phenotype.

In any case, the Havanese is, above all (and outside any hypotheses concerning its origin), the sum of a great variety of antecedents—as are Cuban people themselves. The Havanese is the Cuban interpretation of the Bichon lapdog so abundant in Europe since the Renaissance. Like the Blanquito de la Habana before it, the Havanese was the pet of the colonial aristocracy until the beginning of the 20th century, when North American tastes were imposed, producing a

change in canine fashion and preference. From that moment on, the Havanese was no longer the indulged mascot of the wealthy and became, instead, the daring and affectionate friend of the common people of the city.

It continued to be bred in Cuba all through the 20th century (especially as a pet) because it remained the preferred dog of the Cuban family. The Havanese's character, so similar to that of its masters, along with the ease with which it can be handled, its extraordinary intelligence and its beautiful coat all contributed to the uninterrupted popularity of the breed as a family companion. During the last quarter of the 20th century, however, its breeding has been notably increased and it has become not just a companion but a valued show dog, enjoying great success because of its grace and happy disposition. During Cuba's all-breed dog shows of 1993 and 1994, two Havanese won, respectively, the titles of Reserve Best in Show and Best Puppy in Show. Another pup of this breed also won the latter title in the 1997 all-breed show held in Havana.

For nearly a decade, the Havanese has been protected by its parent club, the Cuban Club of the Bichon Havanese (CCBH). Officially founded by the author in 1991, the CCBH established a rigorous genetic program designed to guarantee the correct

Bred in Germany, this irresistible darling is Sandra Block's Brilliance Belissima. She couldn't be more beautiful.

A famous male Havanese from Finland is Cikitata Uno Gizmo. Havanese have proven excellent show dogs in Cuba as well as on the Continent and in America.

development of the Havanese and set breeding lines under the affix "de la Giraldilla," which is the symbol of Havana. The CCBH is a member of the Federación Cinológica de Cuba, or Cuban Kennel Club, which, in turn, belongs to the Fédération Cynologique Internationale (FCI).

The popularity of this breed grows constantly in Cuba, its native country, where its profusion is in curious contrast to the scarcity of the Havanese in the rest of the world.

THE HAVANESE IN AMERICA
Cuba and the United States maintained a close relationship during the first half of the 20th century. Given the number of Cubans who lived in the United States during the colonial period and the incidence of American residency on the island after that, the Havanese was probably known in the North

This happy Havanese is a companion and show dog.

The growing popularity of the Havanese in the United States can be attributed to the breed's endearing personality, its excellent health and its good looks.

from the turn of the century or before. Nevertheless, systematic breeding of the Havanese in the United States began only in the 1970s.

After the success of the Socialist Revolution in Cuba in the 1960s, many wealthy Cubans migrated from the island to the southern United States and other nearby countries such as Puerto Rico and Costa Rica. Some of them took along their dogs, including the Havanese, as a lively reminder of their native land. With time, these Cuban emigrants began to implant their culture and tastes in their new homelands—especially in Florida, where most of the Cuban refugees settled. Because of the numbers of Cubans, the impact of their

customs and lifestyle on American society was much greater than ever before. Visiting Florida today, the Cuban influence is profound, both in culture and language.

This infusion of Cuban culture resulted in the fortunate situation in which a US breeder named Dorothy Goodale learned of the existence of the Havanese Intrigued and fascinated, Mrs. Goodale began to seek more info mation on this canine breed she had never heard of before, one that offered an alternative to the big dogs she had preferred to breed when she was younger. Sh decided to advertise in a Miami paper in order to locate speci-

The Havanese has existed in America since the mid-1970s. As many Cubans have gone to the States to live, more and more interest in the Havanese has spread. This Havanese *señorita* is ready for a night on the town.

mens of the little dog, and it was through these advertisements that she found two or three immigrant families who had brought their Havanese from Cuba to the United States. From them, Mrs. Goodale succeeded in acquiring six Havanese with pedigrees: a bitch with four female pups and a young unrelated male. A little later, she was able to obtain five more males from a Cuban who was moving from Costa Rica to

Texas and couldn't manage to maintain his canine family.

An experienced breeder, Mrs. Goodale began working with the 11 Havanese she had obtained, using the breed standard published by the FCI. Her first Havanese lines appeared in 1974 and were an immediate success in attracting other breeders. In 1979, Dorothy Goodale, with her husband Bert and a group of collaborators, founded the

Havanese bred in the US today differ significantly from the present-day Cuban dogs, though the American type has improved steadily.

United States: that of the Original Havanese Club of America and that of the Havanese Club of America (which is that approved by the AKC). The two are very similar and quite close to the Cuban standard. In Europe, the FCI and the English Kennel Club each have its own standard.

With the passage of time and the increased number of Havanese in the United States, breeders there began exporting them to Europe. Now the Havanese is known in various European countries and is rapidly gaining popularity, as much for its exoticism as for the qualities that make it not only a pretty show dog but also an excellent companion and watchdog.

It should be noted, however, that reproduction of the Havanese outside Cuba has somewhat weakened the homogeneity and correct type. After all, breeding in the United States began with a very limited genetic pool and this has been the case all along due to the impossibility of acquiring dogs originating in Cuba, the real base of the breed and an unlimited genetic pool.

This history of the Havanese in the United States ends on a positive note, for the breed was recognized by the American Kennel Club, and competes in the Toy Group, with the Havanese Club of America as the AKC parent club.

Havanese Club of America for those interested in breeding and owning Havanese.

In 1991, the United Kennel Club in the U.S. announced its recognition of the Havanese and accepted any dogs registered by the Goodales. The Havanese Club of America was granted recognition by the American Kennel Club (AKC) in 1996.

Meanwhile, the original club split. Dorothy Goodale and some friends reformed as the Original Havanese Club of America, while the other group continued as the Havanese Club of America.

In developing her Havanese lines, Mrs. Goodale followed the FCI standard approved in 1963, which recognized the breed as Cuban, but, with time, she considered it necessary to modify that breed standard and did so. Two standards now exist in the

The Barbet of France is a poodle-like breed with a moderate following on the Continent. The Barbet is believed to be the forerunner of the Poodle, probably one of France's most ancient breeds. It is therefore a likely contributor to the Bichon breeds as well.

CHARACTERISTICS OF THE
HAVANESE

THE FAMILY IS GROWING: YOU NOW HAVE A HAVANESE!

So you've decided you want a dog. Maybe you already know what that means... maybe not.

If you've never had one of these delightful animals, you should know that a dog requires your attention and effort. He needs to be fed, trained, bathed, groomed, systematically wormed and vaccinated, occasionally treated by a vet, regularly exercised and consistently loved. If you aren't willing to face all this, it's best to think twice, because a live animal is not a toy. Without proper care, it can become a troublesome burden instead of what a dog essentially is: a source of enjoyment, affection and entertainment.

Let's assume, though, that you're willing and ready...and that you've just acquired a Havanese. You won't regret it, I assure you. The Havanese is amazingly intelligent, lively, playful and very devoted to his owners. He will immediately show his affection for you and yours (including the children) and, from the moment you bring it home, become a part of your family life.

Of course, you have to keep in mind that this endearing little dog is at his best when his coat is correctly maintained and his body and character are fully developed. A Havanese whose coat is dirty, matted or clipped (for the convenience of owners who aren't prepared to devote the necessary time to his grooming) is not a pretty dog. With an adequate diet and sufficient exercise, your pet will develop the strong bones and muscles that are characteristic of a healthy, beautiful animal.

Finally, a Havanese that is over-indulged, as well as one that is ignored or maltreated,

There can be no doubt that the Havanese is one of the world's most devoted companion animals. Havanese live for your every word and gesture.

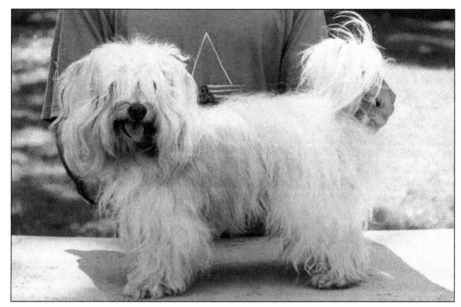

No home is complete without a Havanese! Do not take the commitment of a Havanese lightly. This dog thrives on your affection and positive energy.

will become either timid or aggressive and hence lose one of his finest features: his natural temperament.

You've taken on a responsibility, but don't be alarmed. You'll be rewarded with memorable moments, and probably, you'll wind up like other owners of this breed, living with two, three or more Havanese. You will also begin recommending them to all your friends and relatives.

ARE YOU A HAVANESE PERSON?

When you spoil your dog or overly stimulate his relatively strong character, you are lessening his delightful personality. The Havanese is born to live in your home and not outdoors or in a kennel; but at the same time, this dog requires plenty of exercise because of his vitality and restlessness. Don't over-indulge your pet, but don't maltreat or reprimand him either. Just let him be.

I have known owners who don't let their Havanese walk. These creatures love to be carried and caressed. Since they respond with appropriately endearing and picturesque gestures, many people can't resist their bewitching ways and wind up turning their Havanese into dolls that can't walk on a leash, much less enjoy a good run in the park. Be strong. Don't let yourself be drawn in by their cajolery—for your own good and theirs.

As beguiling and bewitching as the Havanese is, you must resist the temptation to spoil your dog. In doing so, you can indeed "spoil" your dog's temperament and reliability.

Pet them, but not so constantly that they become clinging. Let them relate to other dogs and other people. Unless you have aggressive dogs or a big breed that can become a real threat to your Havanese, don't overprotect him from the others. He can take care of himself. If you become the protector, various problems can arise. Your Havanese will become timid, unable to get along with other dogs. Possibly, if you have an excellent-quality Havanese, on the day you decide to mate him, you'll find that he rejects his mate with indifference or aggression. This is especially important in males. When they are over-socialized with people and don't know how to relate to other dogs, they can't adequately express their virile tendencies.

It really isn't good for a dog to live alone, isolated from other dogs. Even after centuries of domestication and a very close relationship with humans—whom your dog will consider a part of his pack—the dog develops his personality only in relation to his fellow creatures. Moreover, other dogs can alleviate his solitude and permit him to communicate fully in his "own language." You probably recall times when you have felt like a fish out of water, perhaps in a foreign country where you had to communicate in another language and adapt to other customs. It was all very interesting, but remember how comfortable it felt to return home, to be able to talk and act naturally? The same thing happens to animals that live only with humans. If the humans know nothing about the language and body signals of dogs, trying to make their dogs understand their own language, it is even more difficult for the dogs. Then, too, dogs have needs that we, as humans, repress rather than understand and satisfy. This is the case with pups that need to chew and, when they destroy their masters' furniture or shoes, they're banned or abandoned. We don't understand that a dog acts that way because he feels alone or because he is teething and has to chew. Nor do we understand that a pup plays with our shoes because he likes the scent of his owner. Since our shoes smell strongly of "us," the dog feels consoled and secure by chewing on them while he is alone.

Your Havanese, with a character all his own, does the things he does for good reason. Owners must make a special effort to

Havanese exactly like mine?" While everyone has perfectly justifiable reasons for loving and adoring their own dog, not every dog is suitable for breeding. Not only can breeding your Havanese be very costly and time-consuming, it can also be very dangerous for the dam (and puppies).

Breeding dogs is a matter for professionals. The breeder must

Havanese can make excellent watchdogs and protectors of your children. Be wary: children must be instructed how to handle the Havanese. It is cruel to allow children to grab and pull the Havanese's hair, ears and limbs.

understand and appreciate their dogs. Don't forget that the Havanese is an intelligent dog, always ready and able to learn new things.

BREEDING YOUR HAVANESE
So many of us are so enamored of our own Havanese that it seems imperative that we breed them. "Who wouldn't want a

be knowledgeable, first of all about the breeding lines with which they're working. Breeders must know the breed standard thoroughly and the faults and virtues of the specimens involved in the mating. Breeders have to know how to fix desirable traits and eliminate undesirable traits; and, naturally, be very clear about their objective.

Born in Havana! Bebita de la Giraldilla, owned by Merita Batista, with her litter. Note that the puppies are born blind and smooth-coated. Whelping and raising a litter is a huge responsibility that should not be assumed by novices.

What could be cuter than a Havanese puppy? Raising young puppies requires the constant attention of the breeder and dam. Like human infants, puppies are dependent on others for everything!

Simply put, the breeder needs a good head and a good eye.

Let's suppose, though, that you don't pretend to be a breeder but that you have an excellent-quality Havanese whom you believe is worthy of reproducing. Your bitch is 18 months old and in her third heat cycle. You have made the decision before your female came into heat so that you could evaluate her physical faults and virtues as well as her temperament. It is always helpful to study your dog's siblings, parents and grandparents so that you have some idea of the genetic material available.

Undoubtedly, you took time to visit a number of males in order to determine which would be the best option for your female.

The male should be essentially masculine, well developed, healthy and well fed. He should be active and self-confident. A timid, nervous Havanese is a defective dog as far as mating is concerned. You want to mate only healthy specimens with good temperaments. You also want to select for your female a male that is satisfactory or better in the features in which she is deficient. You must choose the best male available, the one most

This six-month-old debutante is A Maiden Effort's Funny Face, owned by German breeder Sandra Block.

At five days old, these Havanese babies are suckling from their mother, Beryll.

representative of the breed type. Make sure he is free of genetic diseases. If possible, try to meet some of his offspring in order to have an idea of what he is producing. Then, and then only, contract with his owner for the mating.

In a general sense, females that are physically and mentally prepared for maternity make good reproducers. Those with a placid temperament and a maternal nature combined with correct conformation are best. Nervous and excitable females, those that are very small and, of course, those with physical or health defects are not suitable.

The ideal age for the first birth is between 15 months and 3 years, while the ideal age for breeding is between 2 and 5 years. This means, that it's most ideal for a Havanese to have a litter between 2 and 3 years of age.

The best way to arrange the mating is by written contract stating the conditions. You can either pay a stud fee or permit the owner of the male to select one or more pups, depending on the size of the litter. Get advice from an experienced breeder on drafting a breeder's agreement

Winning in the show ring is the universally accepted way of proving breeding value. A champion Havanese male will be greatly in demand as a sire for suitable bitches. This prize-winning sire is Cikitata Uno Gizmo of Finland.

and on the choice of the stud.

Usually, the owner of the bitch takes her to the home of the stud, where all the conditions for this visit have been previously coordinated to facilitate the mating. This means that, as soon as the bitch is in heat, her owner should advise the owner of the stud to specify the date of mating.

The reproduction cycle of female dogs normally occurs twice a year. The symptoms are inflammation of the vulva and bleeding, which continues for about ten days. When bleeding stops, the moment for mating arrives. In any case, it's best to consult your veterinarian so that everything turns out the way you want.

The site of the mating should be a tranquil, isolated spot where the dogs won't be overexcited by outside stimuli. Two matings on different days are ideal. Real coupling occurs when the dogs are physically joined end to end for between 10 and 30 minutes.

The gestation period ranges from 59 to 64 days, which makes it vitally important to record the exact dates of the matings. In that way, you will know the probable day of birth and be able to prepare for it properly.

When your bitch is ready to give birth, find her a quiet place where she can be alone and where you can watch her. If you

Whelping and rearing a litter is hard work for the dam, too! She has to attend to her litter 24 hours a day for 10 to 12 weeks. Don't neglect the dam's needs: she will need attention, a special diet and ample opportunity for exercise (away from the litter).

Puppies in their first week of life do little more than sleep and eat. The breeder must take care that all the puppies are nursing sufficiently and that the dam isn't neglecting any particular baby.

lack experience in these matters, keep in touch with your vet before and during birth. Generally, the mother births her pups by herself without any problem, but certain factors may have a negative influence, such as fussing and handling by her owners, noise and movement in the birthing area, small pelvic capacity or very big pups. There are cases where the bitch births her pups surrounded by the family, which can make her nervous to the point of inhibiting the birth.

Don't permit her to give birth on rags or cloths. It is better to

use old newspapers that can be changed constantly as the birth continues.

Once the birth is over, watch the mother discreetly. Keep her where she's quiet and within sight. Sometimes, without meaning to, the mother will lie down on a pup and asphyxiate it or she might decide to move the pups to another and less appropriate spot, such as under the bed. Make sure the mother has milk and that all the pups are nursing normally. A healthy Havanese litter is cause for celebration. The breeder's hard work and preparation reap wonderful furry rewards. The proud breeder in Havana passes out only the best cigars upon the whelping of a beautiful litter of puppies. (That's a distinct advantage of the Havanese!)

The average Havanese litter is three or four pups, although litters of six or even seven are not uncommon. The puppy's color at birth is seldom the same as when it reaches adulthood for, with the exception of white or light

beige, the color will probably be diluted. Black pups, for example, often grow up to be gray, while brown or red pups may turn out to be beige or ivory. A black and white pup may remain the same or become gray and white. The matter of color is genetic, of course. Nevertheless, a Havanese breeder should not breed for color, but rather for soundness, conformation and temperament. Though useful in relation to pigmentation, color is only an esthetic element and does not determine the dog's quality.

This is not the place to go into detail about raising pups. We simply want to note that, after three weeks, you can begin to give the little ones solid food in order to help the mother wean them and teach them how to eat. The vet can recommend the appropriate food, indicate when

At eight weeks of age, this litter seems fairly ready to take on the world. This is the first litter bred by breeder Sandra Block of Germany.

and how to worm them and, later, vaccinate them properly according to age.

Most importantly, we urge you not to reproduce dogs capriciously. Before you even think of mating your dog, determine whether her pups will have the future they deserve. Mate exclusively with those specimens that can reproduce quality. Any other course will be a detriment to the development of the breed you appreciate so much.

Your Havanese is a remarkable gift! Never take your dog for granted. Be firm in your commitment to own a Havanese, and give him the best life you can.

LIFE WITH A DOG
Life is a privilege. A dog is a marvelous form of life. For many centuries, this creature has been our friend and confidante, showering us with loyalty and love without asking whether we really deserve it, accepting us as we are without judging us. All this is much more than we can ever expect of another human being.

Having a Havanese is a highly gratifying and healthy experience. Science has documented over and over again the beneficial effects pets have on our physical and mental health. For this reason, the Havanese is one of the breeds used in therapy work. Owners of Havanese bring their dogs to nursing homes and rehab facilities to visit the sick and aged. The Havanese brightens the spirit of thousands of people around the world.

A dog is also a lesson for any attentive owner who allows himself to be influenced by his pet's natural wisdom. We should be able to treat him as he treats us. Never maltreat him. Don't neglect him. And, above all do not abandon him.

A Havanese can establish such a close link with his human friend that it's sometimes hard to tell who's who in this relationship. And the dog may not be able to survive being separated from the owner he loves. For that reason, we have to think carefully before we decide to acquire a dog. A dog is a responsibility we cannot reject under any circumstances. "We are responsible for what we domesticate," said Saint-Exupéry's Little Prince, and he was right.

Make your Havanese a part of your life. Provide fun opportunities to exercise and socialize for your dog. He will become a more well-rounded and loving companion. The author and two other owners are walking their dogs on the Malacon, a popular thoroughfare in Havana. The sea is to the left.

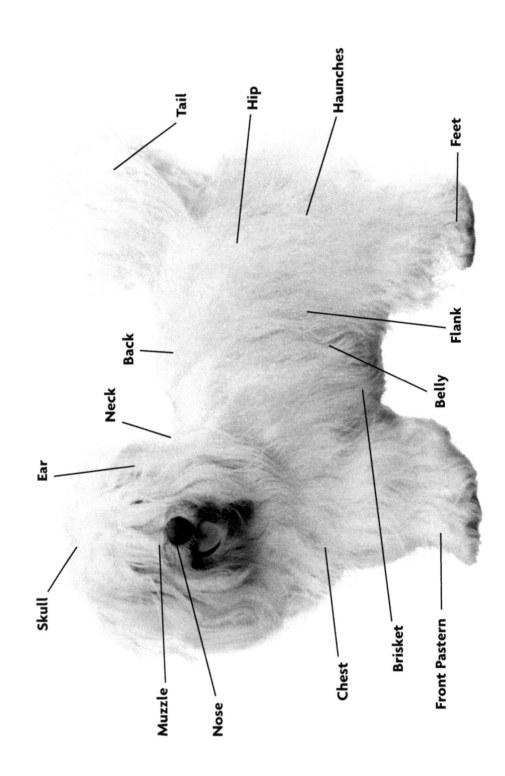

Tail

Hip

Haunches

Feet

Back

Neck

Flank

Ear

Belly

Skull

Chest

Brisket

Muzzle

Nose

Front Pastern

HAVANESE

The following description is based on the FCI's breed standard, the standard of the breed's homeland, and gives the traits of the ideal representative of the Havanese. The breed standard is the measuring stick by which breeders breed and judges judge. For the average pet owner, the standard gives all of the important features that the breed should possess, from body type and color to coat texture and temperament. As standards vary from country to country those wishing to show their dogs with the AKC should familiarize themselves with the AKC standard.

WHAT THE HAVANESE SHOULD LOOK AND ACT LIKE

HEAD

The head is proportional to the size of the body, with a broad, flattened skull and moderate nasal-frontal depression. The muzzle is slightly longer than the forehead and the stop is moderate but perfectly visible. Its large, dark, expressive, almond-shaped eyes are surrounded by a halo of pigmentation. The nose is pronounced, tapered and black; the mouth is ample with fine,

black lips. The underjaw is flat and firm. Teeth meet in a scissors bite. The medium-sized ears are broad-based and implanted slightly above eye level. They fall to a point without covering the cheeks. The ears have a slight dip that rises when the dog is at attention, giving this breed its unusual look of alertness. Long hair falls from the occiput over the muzzle, covering the eyes, which are barely visible behind this sunshade.

The head should be broad with a flat skull, adorned with long hair, creating a sunshade over the eyes—ideal for a dog living in sunny Cuba.

The body should be somewhat longer than tall. The torso is covered with long, silky hair.

NECK

Moderately long and erect, with no dewlap.

BODY

The Havanese is somewhat longer than it is tall. The flanks are firm and rounded, the haunches high and the back strong, with the spine sloping slightly toward the rump. The sternum line coincides with elbow height. The torso is covered with abundant, silky hair—often 4 inches long in this zone and a little longer on the chest than on the stomach—which never reaches the ground.

FOREQUARTERS

Short, straight and moderately angled. Longitude from feet to elbows is the same as from elbows to withers. Leg bones are strong, feet rounded and the hair is shorter here than on the torso.

HINDQUARTERS

Solidly muscular thighs with a convex outer edge. Viewed from the rear, the legs are perfectly straight and strongly boned with moderately angled joints. The feet are oval-shaped. The hindquarters are covered with profuse, undulating hair.

TAIL

Set high, the tail is thick at the base and tapers to a point as it curves over the rump like a plume, without touching the body. If the tail is too close to the body or curly, it destroys the harmony and correct image of the Havanese, especially its walk.

SKIN

Tight to the body, wrinkle-free and cream-colored.

COAT

The beauty of the Havanese is in its coat, which should be abundant over the entire body. The hair is fine, long and undulating, with a very typical pearly sheen. The hair on the paws is shorter than on the body.

COLOR

Any color or combination of colors is acceptable in the Havanese, though, as we have already noted, the most common colors are ivory or champagne.

A young Cuban Havanese puppy named Magico, shaping up nicely for the show ring. The puppy coat is replaced by the adult coat by around eight months of age. This puppy's coat will become lighter as he matures.

HEIGHT

Height at the withers can range from 9 to 12 inches (23 to 30 cm), but the ideal is 10.5 inches (27 cm).

MOVEMENT

The Havanese should move freely and easily, with a lively, elegant gait. The head is held high and the tail movement conveys will and pride.

FAULTS

Incorrect bite: overshot, under-shot or clamp bite. Crooked bones. Poor pigmentation. Corkscrew tail. Timidity.

The Havanese standard does not make a smile mandatory, but it sure does reveal the breed's joy of life.

CHARACTER

The temperament of the Havanese plays a decisive role in its form. These dogs should be neither timid nor aggressive. By character, the breed is lively, intelligent and up to any situation. It shows no cowardice, in spite of its size. It enjoys sharing with its family every kind of inside or outside activity, from swimming, running to romping in the grass or in the snow. Its joy in life and its sense of innate pride are clearly expressed in its movements and in how it carries its head and tail. It gets along well with others of the same breed and even other breeds; for, although the Havanese is somewhat dominant, it's not a quarrelsome dog.

The FCI breed standard describes the Havanese's look of alertness as well as its innate pride and vivacity, evident in the breed's carriage and movement.

The skull is broad and flat. The stop is moderate but perfectly visible.

The eyes are dark and almond shaped, surrounded by dark pigmentation (shown on the far right).

The nose is entirely black, without blotchy pink pigmentation (Dudley nose, shown on the right).

The body and head are profusely covered with long silky hair, giving the dog a natural, "ungroomed" appearance. The tail curves up like a plume.

The longitude from feet to elbows is the same as from elbows to withers. The hair on the chest is longer than on the stomach.

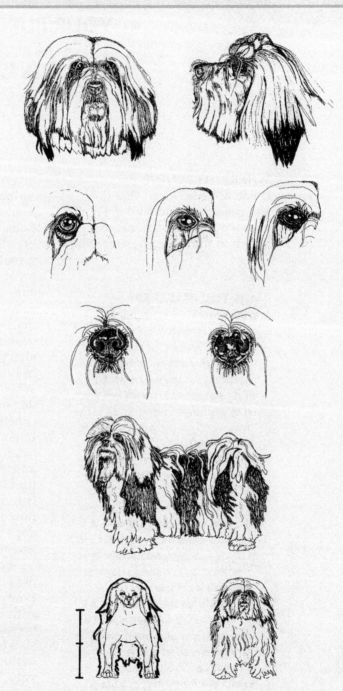

HAVANESE

WHERE TO BEGIN?

If you are convinced that the Havanese is the ideal dog for you, it's time to learn about where to find a puppy and what to look for. We recommend very seriously to anyone interested in acquiring a Havanese outside Cuba that he investigate the breeder's bloodlines for possible genetic diseases, of which progressive retinal atrophy (PRA) and cataracts are great concerns. Responsible breeders screen their dogs for these possible problems and never include an affected dog or possible carrier in their breeding program. Whether you are seeking a pet dog or show dog, freedom from genetic diseases is of paramount importance. Both PRA and cataracts can lead to blindness in an afflicted Havanese. You will find it useful, when looking for a Havanese, to listen to the opinion of registries that have lists of dogs that are clear of certain genetic diseases.

Locating a litter of Havanese hopefully should not present a problem for the new owner. Although this is a relatively new breed in the US, you should be able to locate reputable breeders within a reasonable distance of your home. You are looking for an established breeder with

ARE YOU PREPARED?

Unfortunately, when a puppy is bought by someone who does not take into consideration the time and attention that dog ownership requires, it is the puppy who suffers when he is either abandoned or placed in a shelter by a frustrated owner. So all of the "homework" you do in preparation for your pup's arrival will benefit you both. The more informed you are, the more you will know what to expect and the better equipped you will be to handle the ups and downs of raising a puppy. Hopefully, everyone in the household is willing to do his part in raising and caring for the pup. The anticipation of owning a dog often brings a lot of promises from excited family members: "I will walk him every day," "I will feed him," "I will house-train him," etc., but these things take time and effort, and promises can easily be forgotten once the novelty of the new pet has worn off.

Be certain that your breeder has screened his stock for eye problems. Your puppy should have dark, clear eyes.

outstanding dog ethics and a strong commitment to the breed. New owners should have as many questions as they have doubts. An established breeder is indeed the one to answer your four million questions and make you comfortable with your choice of the Havanese. An established breeder will sell you a puppy at a fair price if, and only if, the breeder determines that you are a suitable, worthy owner of his dogs. An established breeder can be relied upon for advice, no matter what time of day or night. A reputable breeder will accept a puppy back, without questions, should you decide that this not the right dog for you.

Choosing a breeder is an important first step in dog ownership. Fortunately, the majority of Havanese breeders are devoted to the breed and its well-being. The American Kennel Club is able to refer you to breeders of quality Havanese, as can the national Havanese clubs and any local or regional breed club. Potential owners are encouraged to attend a dog show to view the Havanese "in the fur," to see what Havanese look like outside a photographer's lens. Provided you approach the handlers when they are not terribly busy with the dogs, most are more than willing to answer questions, recommend breeders and give advice.

Once you have contacted and met a breeder or two and made your choice about which breeder is best suited to your needs, it's time to visit the litter. Keep in mind that many quality breeders have waiting lists. Sometimes new owners have to wait as long as two years for a puppy. If you are really committed to the breeder whom you've selected, then you will wait (and hope for an early arrival!). If not, you may have to resort to your second- or third-choice breeder. Don't be too anxious, however. If the breeder doesn't have any waiting list, or any customers, there is probably a good reason. Since the Havanese produces small litters, breeders have great

TEMPERAMENT COUNTS

Your selection of a good puppy can be determined by your needs. A show potential or a good pet? It is your choice. Every puppy, however, should be of good temperament. Although show-quality puppies are bred and raised with emphasis on physical conformation, responsible breeders strive for equally good temperament. Do not buy from a breeder who concentrates solely on physical beauty at the expense of personality.

In Spanish, we call puppies *perritos* or *cachorros!* These pups are only three weeks old.

demand for their precious commodity. When observing the pups, beware of the shy or overly aggressive puppy: be especially conscious of the nervous Havanese pup. Don't let sentiment or emotion trap you into buying the runt of the litter.

Surely the color of some Havanese in this book has attracted your eye. Many newcomers to the Havanese have strong prejudices toward one color or another. In reality, color in this breed has little bearing on the dog. The breed standard indicates no preference for color, and that open mindset should extend to pet selection as well. New owners should concern themselves with soundness of temperament and construction as

PUPPY APPEARANCE

Your puppy should have a well-fed appearance but not a distended abdomen, which may indicate worms or incorrect feeding, or both. The body should be firm, with a solid feel. The skin of the abdomen should be pale pink and clean, without signs of scratching or rash. Check the hind legs to see if the dewclaws were removed, if any were present at birth.

Three "fine dogs" setting a new fashion trend in the canine world. For many years in Cuba, the Havanese was incorrectly called Maltese. The bitches above are (l to r) Dolly and Epoca de la Giraldilla, owned by the Carbonell family, and Esmeralda de la Giraldilla.

well as freedom from congenital diseases. Although the black Havanese or the blonde Havanese captures your eye, for your heart's sake choose your puppy with your mind! Health, stable temperament, proper structure make for an ideal Havanese choice.

Always check the bite of your selected puppy to be sure that it is neither overshot or undershot. This may not be too noticeable on a young puppy, but

PEDIGREE VS. REGISTRATION CERTIFICATE

Too often new owners are confused between these two important documents. Your puppy's pedigree, essentially a family tree, is a written record of a dog's genealogy of three generations or more. The pedigree will show you the names as well as performance titles of all dogs in your pup's background. Your breeder must provide you with a registration application, with his part properly filled out. You must complete the application and send it to the AKC with the proper fee. Every puppy must come from a litter that has been AKC-registered by the breeder, born in the USA and from a sire and dam that are also registered with the AKC.

The seller must provide you with complete records to identify the puppy. The AKC requires that the seller provide the buyer with the following: breed; sex, color and markings; date of birth; litter number (when available); names and registration numbers of the parents; breeder's name; and date sold or delivered.

it is a fairly common problem with certain lines of Havanese.

Breeders commonly allow visitors to see the litter by around the fifth or sixth week, and puppies leave for their new homes around the tenth week, rarely before. Breeders who permit their puppies to leave early are more interested in a profit than in their puppies' well-being. Puppies need to learn the rules of the trade from their dams, and most dams continue teaching the pups manners, and dos and don'ts until around the tenth week. Breeders spend significant amounts of time with the Havanese toddlers so that they are able to interact with the "other species," i.e., humans. Given the long history that dogs and humans have, bonding between the two species is natural but must be nurtured. A well-bred, well-socialized Havanese pup wants nothing more than to be near you and please you.

COMMITMENT OF OWNERSHIP

After considering all of these factors, you have most likely already made some very important decisions about selecting your puppy. You have chosen a Havanese, which means that you have decided which characteristics you want in a dog and what

If you are interested in seeing Havanese, attend a dog show to view the dogs in action, in this case, Ambar D' Sirius, a Cuban champion. It's a great place to meet breeders and owners and to make essential contacts.

type of dog will best fit into your family and lifestyle. If you have selected a breeder, you have gone a step further—you have done your research and found a responsible, conscientious person who breeds quality Havaneses and who should be a reliable source of help as you and your puppy adjust to life together. If you have observed a litter in action, you have

TIME TO GO HOME

Breeders should not release Havanese puppies until they are at least ten weeks of age. Some breeders of Toy breeds keep their puppies a little longer, not releasing them until around 12 weeks, given their petite sizes. If a breeder has a puppy that is 12 weeks of age or older, he is likely well socialized and house-trained. Be sure that he is otherwise healthy before deciding to take him home.

Choose the puppy from the litter that exudes the most happiness and personality. This dam is Blanquita de la Giraldilla. Never take home the sad, timid puppy out of sympathy.

obtained a firsthand look at the dynamics of a puppy "pack" and, thus, you should have learned about each pup's individual personality—perhaps you have even found one that particularly appeals to you.

However, even if you have not yet found the Havanese puppy of your dreams, observing pups will help you learn to recognize certain behavior and to determine what a pup's behavior indicates about his temperament. You will be able to pick out which pups are the leaders, which ones are less outgoing, which ones are confident, which ones are shy, playful, friendly, etc. Equally as important, you will learn to recognize what a healthy pup should look and act like. All of these things will help you in your search, and when you find the Havanese that was meant for you, you will know it!

Researching your breed, selecting a responsible breeder

YOUR SCHEDULE . . .
If you lead an erratic, unpredictable life, with daily or weekly changes in your work requirements, consider the problems of owning a puppy. The new puppy has to be fed regularly, socialized (loved, petted, handled, introduced to other people) and, most importantly, allowed to go outdoors for house-training. As the dog gets older, he can be more tolerant of deviations in his feeding and relief schedule.

and observing as many pups as possible are all important steps on the way to dog ownership. It may seem like a lot of effort...and you have not even brought the pup home yet! Remember, though, you cannot be too careful when it comes to deciding on the type of dog you want and finding out about your prospective pup's background. Buying a puppy is not—or should not be—just another whimsical purchase. This is one instance in which you actually do get to choose your own family! You may be thinking that buying a puppy should be fun— it should not be so serious and so much work. Keep in mind that your puppy is not a cuddly stuffed toy or decorative lawn

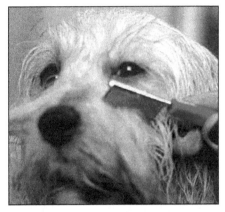

While the Havanese appears to be an easy-care, no-maintenance dog, his hallmark silky coat requires some time and energy from his owner.

ornament, but a creature that will become a real member of your family. You will come to realize that, while buying a puppy is a pleasurable and exciting endeavor, it is not something to be taken lightly. Relax...the fun will start when the pup comes home!

Always keep in mind that a puppy is nothing more than a baby in a furry disguise...a baby who is virtually helpless in a human world and who trusts his owner for fulfillment of his basic needs for survival. In addition to food, water and shelter, your pup needs care, protection, guidance and love. If you are not prepared

Are you willing to devote the proper time to keep your Havanese looking his absolute best?

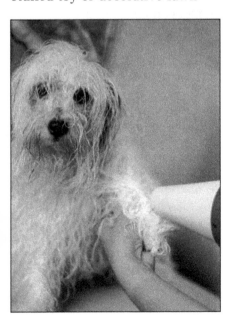

ARE YOU A FIT OWNER?
If the breeder from whom you are buying a puppy asks you a lot of personal questions, do not be insulted. Such a breeder wants to be sure that you will be a fit provider for his puppy.

to commit to this, then you are not prepared to own a dog.

"Wait a minute," you say. "How hard could this be? All of my neighbors own dogs and they seem to be doing just fine. Why should I have to worry about all of this?" Well, you should not worry about it; in fact, you will probably find that once your Havanese pup gets used to his new home, he will fall into his place in the family quite naturally. But it never hurts to emphasize the commitment of dog ownership. With some time and patience, it is really not too difficult to raise a curious and exuberant Havanese pup to be a well-adjusted and well-mannered adult dog—a dog that could be your most loyal friend.

PREPARING PUPPY'S PLACE IN YOUR HOME
Researching your breed and finding a breeder are only two aspects of the homework you will have to do before bringing your Havanese puppy home. You will also have to prepare your home and family for the new addition. Much as you would prepare a nursery for a newborn baby, you will need to designate a place in your home that will be the puppy's own. How you prepare your home will depend on how much freedom the dog will be allowed. Whatever you decide, you must ensure that he has a place that he can "call his own."

When you bring your new puppy into your home, you are bringing him into what will become his home as well. Obviously, you did not buy a puppy so that he could take control of your house, but in order for a puppy to grow into a stable, well-adjusted dog, he has to feel comfortable in his surroundings. Remember, he is leaving the warmth and security of his mother and littermates, as well as the familiarity of the only place he has ever known, so it is important to make his transition as easy as possible. By preparing a place in your home for the puppy, you are making him feel as welcome as possible in a strange new place. It should not take him long to get used to it, but the sudden shock of being transplanted is somewhat traumatic for a young pup. Imagine how a small child would feel in the same situation—that is how your puppy must be feeling. It is

QUALITY FOOD
The cost of food must be mentioned. All dogs need a good-quality food with an adequate supply of protein to develop their bones and muscles properly. Most dogs are not picky eaters but, unless fed properly, can quickly succumb to skin problems.

up to you to reassure him and to let him know, "Little fellow, you are going to like it here!"

WHAT YOU SHOULD BUY

CRATE

To someone unfamiliar with the use of crates in dog training, it may seem like punishment to shut a dog in a crate, but this is at least debatable. Most professional breeders and trainers are recommending crates as preferred tools for pet puppies as well as show puppies. They argue that crates are not cruel—

Crates can be purchased at your local pet shop. Crate training is a popular innovation in dog care. Top breeders around the world are convinced that crate training is the best way to housebreak and train a dog. Your pet shop will offer a variety of sizes, styles and colors.

PHOTO COURTESY OF MIKKI PET PRODUCTS.

CRATE-TRAINING TIPS

During crate training, you should partition off the section of the crate in which the pup stays. If he is given too big an area, this will hinder your training efforts. Crate training is based on the fact that a dog does not like to soil his sleeping quarters, so it is ineffective to keep a pup in an area that is so big that he can eliminate in one end and get far enough away from it to sleep. Also, you want to make the crate den-like for the pup. Blankets and a favorite toy will make the crate cozy for the small pup; as he grows, you may want to evict some of his "roommates" to make more room. It will take some coaxing at first, but be patient. Given some time to get used to it, your pup will adapt to his new home-within-a-home quite nicely.

and have many humane and highly effective uses in dog care and training. For example, crate training is a very popular and very successful housebreaking method. A crate can keep your dog safe during travel and, perhaps most importantly, a crate provides your dog with a place of his own in your home. It serves as a "doggie bedroom" of sorts—your Havanese can curl up in his crate when he wants to sleep or when he just needs a

break. Many dogs sleep in their crates overnight. When lined with soft bedding and with his favorite toy inside, a crate becomes a cozy pseudo-den for your dog. Like his ancestors, he too will seek out the comfort and retreat of a den—especially if the door is left open so he can go in and out of his own accord.

As far as purchasing a crate, the type that you buy is up to you. It will most likely be one of the two most popular types: wire or fiberglass. There are advantages and disadvantages to each type. For example, a wire crate is more open, allowing the air to flow through and affording the dog a view of what is going on

Special delivery! A Havanese puppy is not a toy. New owners must be prepared to accommodate the young pup with everything he needs to live.

(FACING PAGE) Provide your Havanese with an appropriately sized crate. In no time, your Havanese will accept his crate as his own den, a place to which he can retire and spend some time by himself.

around him while a fiberglass crate is sturdier. Both can double as travel crates, providing protection for the dog in the car. A medium-size crate is the best choice for the Havanese, who can stand up to 12 inches at the shoulder at his mature height.

BEDDING

A lambswool crate pad in the dog's crate will help the dog feel more at home and you may also like to give him a small blanket. This will take the place of the leaves, twigs, etc., that the pup would use in the wild to make a den; the pup can make his own "burrow" in the crate. Although your pup is far removed from his den-making ancestors, the denning instinct is still a part of his genetic makeup. Second, until you bring your pup home, he has been sleeping amid the warmth of his mother and littermates, and while a blanket is not the same as a warm, breathing

Your pet shop will carry many essential items for your Havanese, including toys, grooming supplies, crates, bowls and more. Dog ownership is an expensive proposition. Can you provide a suitable home for a Havanese?

body, it still provides heat and something with which to snuggle. You will want to wash your pup's bedding frequently in case he has an accident in his crate, and replace or remove any blanket or pad that becomes ragged and starts to fall apart.

Toys

Toys are a must for dogs of all ages, especially for curious playful pups. Puppies are the "children" of the dog world, and what child does not love toys? Chew toys provide enjoyment to both dog and owner—your dog will enjoy playing with his favorite toys, while you will enjoy the fact that they distract him from your expensive shoes and leather sofa. Puppies love to chew; in fact, chewing is a physical need for pups as they are teething, and everything looks appetizing! The full range of your possessions—

Pet shops offer a wide selection of suitable dog toys that your Havanese will welcome. Never offer your dog toys that are manufactured for children as they may be dangerous to a teething puppy.

from old dishcloth to Oriental rug—are fair game in the eyes of a teething pup. Puppies are not all that discerning when it comes to finding something to literally "sink their teeth into"—everything tastes great!

Breeders advise owners to resist stuffed toys, because they can become de-stuffed in no time. The overly excited pup may ingest the stuffing, which is neither digestible nor nutritious. Similarly, squeaky toys are quite popular, but should be avoided for the Havanese. Perhaps a squeaky toy can be used as an aid in training, but not for free play. If a pup "disembowels" one

TOYS, TOYS, TOYS!

With a big variety of dog toys available, and so many that look like they would be a lot of fun for a dog, be careful in your selection. It is amazing what a set of puppy teeth can do to an innocent-looking toy, so, obviously, safety is a major consideration. Be sure to choose the most durable products that you can find. Hard nylon bones and toys are a safe bet, and many of them are offered in different scents and flavors that will be sure to capture your dog's attention. It is always fun to play a game of fetch with your dog, and there are balls and flying discs that are specially made to withstand dog teeth.

of these, the small plastic squeaker inside can be dangerous if swallowed. Monitor the condition of all your pup's toys carefully and get rid of any that have been chewed to the point of becoming potentially dangerous.

Be careful of natural bones, which have a tendency to splinter into sharp, dangerous pieces. Also be careful of rawhide, which can turn into pieces that are easy to swallow or into a mushy mess on your carpet.

LEAD

A nylon lead is probably the best option, as it is the most resistant

Most trainers recommend using a lightweight nylon leash for your Havanese. Pet shops offer dozens of choices of collars and leashes, in different styles, colors and lengths.

to puppy teeth should your pup take a liking to chewing on his lead. Of course, this is a habit that should be nipped in the bud, but, if your pup likes to chew on his lead, he has a very slim chance of being able to chew through the strong nylon. Nylon leads are also lightweight, which is good for a young Havanese who is just getting used to the idea of walking on a lead. For everyday walking and safety purposes, the nylon lead is a good choice. As your pup grows up and gets used to walking on the lead, you may want to purchase a flexible lead. These leads allow you to extend the length to give the dog a broader area to explore or to shorten the length to keep the close to you.

COLLAR

Your pup should get used to wearing a collar outside the house since you will want to attach his ID tags to it. Plus, you have to attach the lead to something! A lightweight nylon collar is a good choice; make sure that it fits snugly enough so that the pup cannot wriggle out of it, but is loose enough so that it will not be uncomfortably tight around the pup's neck. You should be able to fit a finger between the pup and the collar. When your Havanese is inside the home, consider removing the collar as it can ruin the coat.

CHOOSE AN APPROPRIATE COLLAR

The **BUCKLE COLLAR** is the standard collar used for everyday purposes. Be sure that you adjust the buckle on growing puppies. Check it every day. It can become too tight overnight! These collars can be made of leather or nylon. Attach your dog's identification tags to this collar.

The **CHOKE COLLAR** is designed for training. It is constructed of highly polished steel so that it slides easily through the stainless steel loop. The idea is that the dog controls the pressure around his neck and he will stop pulling if the collar becomes uncomfortable. A chain choke collar is not suitable for use on the Havanese. Cloth or leather collars are gentler on the dog and the coat. *Never* leave this collar on your dog when not training.

The **HALTER** is for a trained dog that has to be restrained to prevent running away, chasing a cat and the like. Considered the most humane of all collars, it is frequently used on smaller dogs on which collars are not comfortable.

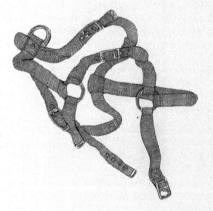

Food and water bowls can be constructed of sturdy plastic, ceramic, clay or stainless steel. Choose durable bowls that can be cleaned easily.

PHOTO COURTESY OF MIKKI PET PRODUCTS.

FOOD AND WATER BOWLS

Your pup will need two bowls, one for food and one for water. You should place an additional bowl outside so that your Havanese can have a cool drink when playing outdoors. Stainless steel or sturdy plastic bowls are popular choices. Plastic bowls are more chewable. Dogs tend not to chew on the steel variety, which can be sterilized. It is important to buy sturdy bowls since anything is in danger of being chewed by puppy teeth and you do not want your dog to be chewing apart his bowl (for his safety and for your wallet!).

CLEANING SUPPLIES

Until a pup is house-trained, you will be doing a lot of cleaning. "Accidents" will occur, which is okay in the beginning because the puppy does not know any better. All you can do is be prepared to clean up any accidents. Old rags, towels, newspapers and a safe disinfectant are good to have on hand.

BEYOND THE BASICS

The items previously discussed are the bare necessities. You will find out what else you need as you go along—grooming supplies, flea/tick protection, baby gates to partition a room, etc. These things will vary depending on your situation, but it is important that you have everything you need to feed and make your Havanese comfortable in his first few days at home.

PUPPY-PROOFING YOUR HOME

Aside from making sure that your Havanese will be comfortable in your home, you also have to make sure that your home is safe for your Havanese. This means taking precautions that your pup will not get into anything he should not get into and that there is nothing within his reach that may harm him should he sniff it, chew it, inspect it, etc. This probably seems obvious since, while you are primarily concerned with your pup's safety, at the same time you do not want your belongings to be ruined. Breakables should be placed out of reach of the area designated for your dog. This area should also be free of any potentially dangerous items. An electrical cord can pose a danger should the puppy decide to taste it—and who is going to convince a pup

that it would not make a great chew toy? Cords should be fastened tightly against the wall, away from puppy teeth. If your dog is going to spend time in a crate, make sure that there is nothing near his crate that he can reach if he sticks his curious little nose or paws through the openings. Just as you would with a child, keep all household cleaners and chemicals where the pup cannot get to them.

It is also important to make sure that outside your home is safe. Of course your puppy should never be unsupervised, but a pup let loose in the yard will want to run and explore, and he should be granted that freedom. Do not let a fence give

Responsible, law-abiding dog owners pick up their dogs' droppings whenever they are in public. Pooper-scooper devices make the job quick and easy.

you a false sense of security; you would be surprised how crafty (and persistent) a dog can be in figuring out how to dig under and squeeze his way through small holes, or to jump or climb over a fence. The remedy is to make the fence high enough so that it really is impossible for your dog to get over it (about 4 feet should suffice), and well embedded into the ground. Be ready. Now all you have to do is collect your Havanese from the breeder and the fun begins, right? Well…not so fast. Something else you need to prepare is your pup's first trip to the vet. You should have an appointment arranged for your pup before you pick him up and plan on taking him for an examination before bringing him home.

Puppies are naturally curious and will attempt to chew on anything they find. Owners should keep all destructible and/or valuable items away from the exploring Havanese pup.

sure to secure any gaps in the fence. Check the fence periodically to ensure that it is in good shape and make repairs as needed; a very determined pup may return to the same spot to "work on it" until he is able to get through.

FIRST TRIP TO THE VET

You have picked out your puppy, and your home and family are

SKULL & CROSSBONES

Thoroughly puppy-proof your house before bringing your puppy home. Never use cockroach or rodent poisons or plant fertilizers in any area accessible to the puppy. Avoid the use of toilet cleaners. Most dogs are born with "toilet-bowl sonar" and will take a drink if the lid is left open. Also keep the trash secured and out of reach.

The pup's first visit will consist of an overall examination to make sure that the pup does not have any problems that are not apparent to you. The vet will also set up a schedule for the pup's vaccinations; the breeder will inform you of which ones the pup has already received and the vet can continue from there.

INTRODUCTION TO THE FAMILY

Everyone in the house will be excited about the puppy's coming home and will want to pet him and play with him, but it is best to make the introductions low-key so as not to overwhelm the puppy. He is apprehensive already. It is the first time he has been separated from his dam and the breeder, and the ride to your home is likely the first time he has been in a car. The last thing you want to do is smother him, as this will only frighten him further. This is not to say that human contact is not extremely necessary at this stage, because this is the time when a connection between the pup and his human family is formed. Gentle petting and soothing words should help console him, as well as just putting him down and letting him explore on his own (under your watchful eye, of course).

The pup may approach the family members or may busy

NATURAL TOXINS
Examine your grass and landscaping before bringing your puppy home. Many varieties of plants have leaves, stems or flowers that are toxic if ingested, and you can depend on a curious puppy to investigate them. Ask your vet for information on poisonous plants or research them at your library.

himself with exploring for a while. Gradually, each person should spend some time with the pup, one at a time, crouching down to get as close to the pup's level as possible and letting him sniff their hands and petting him gently. He definitely needs human attention and he needs to be touched—this is how to form an immediate bond. Just remember that the pup is experiencing a lot of things for the first time, at the same time. There are new people, new noises, new smells and new things to investigate, so be gentle, be affectionate and be as comforting as you can be.

YOUR PUP'S FIRST NIGHT HOME

You have traveled home with your new charge safely in his basket or crate. He's been to the vet for a thorough check-up; he's been weighed, his papers examined; perhaps he's even been vaccinated and wormed as well.

He's met the family, licked the whole family, including the excited children and the less-than-happy cat. He's explored his area, his new bed, the yard and anywhere else he's been permitted. He's eaten his first meal at home and relieved himself in the proper place. He's heard lots of new sounds, smelled new friends and seen more of the outside world than ever before.

That was just the first day! He's worn out and is ready for bed...or so you think!

It's puppy's first night and you are ready to say "Good night"—keep in mind that this is

THE RIDE HOME
Taking your dog from the breeder to your home in a car can be a very uncomfortable experience for both of you. The puppy will have been taken from his warm, friendly, safe environment and brought into a strange new environment—an environment that moves! Be prepared for loose bowels, urination, crying, whining and even fear biting. With proper love and encouragement when you arrive home, the stress of the trip should quickly disappear.

Your Havanese family is growing and growing! Even experienced owners can find the first night with a new Havanese puppy stressful. Mother, daughter and grand-daughter: Dolly, Epoca and Blanquita de la Giraldilla, with a pup from Blanquita's litter.

puppy's first night ever to be sleeping alone. His dam and littermates are no longer at paw's length and he's a bit scared, cold and lonely. Be reassuring to your new family member, but this is not the time to spoil him and give in to his inevitable whining.

Puppies whine. They whine to let others know where they are and hopefully to get company out of it. Place your pup in his new bed or crate in his room and close the door. Mercifully, he may fall asleep without a peep. When the inevitable occurs, ignore the whining; he is fine. Be strong and keep his interest in mind. Do not allow your heart to become guilty and visit the pup. He will fall asleep eventually.

Many breeders recommend placing a piece of bedding from

his former home in his new bed so that he recognizes the scent of his littermates. Others still advise placing a hot water bottle in his bed for warmth. This latter may be a good idea provided the pup doesn't attempt to suckle— he'll get good and wet and may not fall asleep so fast.

Puppy's first night can be somewhat stressful for the pup and his new family. Remember that you are setting the tone of nighttime at your house. Unless you want to play with your pup every night at 10 p.m., midnight and 2 a.m., don't initiate the habit. Your family will thank you, and soon so will your pup!

Conformation is hard to evaluate at such a young age, but a pup should have a sound, not square body. The puppy coat will change and grow into the adult's long, silky hair.

PREVENTING PUPPY PROBLEMS

SOCIALIZATION
Now that you have done all of the preparatory work and have helped your pup get accustomed

FEEDING TIPS

You will probably start feeding your pup the same food that he has been getting from the breeder; the breeder should give you a few days' supply to start you off. Although you should not give your pup too many treats, you will want to have puppy treats on hand for coaxing, training, rewards, etc. Be careful, though, as a small pup's calorie requirements are relatively low and a few treats can add up to almost a full day's worth of calories without the required nutrition.

A basket with soft padding is an excellent choice for the new puppy. Offer the puppy a safe chew toy to take to his new bed.

to his new home and family, it is about time for you to have some fun! Socializing your Havanese pup gives you the opportunity to show off your new friend, and your pup gets to reap the benefits of being an adorable furry creature that people will want to pet and, in general, think is absolutely precious!

Besides getting to know his new family, your puppy should be exposed to other people, animals and situations, but of course he must not come into close contact with dogs you

STRESS-FREE

Some experts in canine health advise that stress during a dog's early years of development can compromise and weaken his immune system, and may trigger the potential for a shortened life. They emphasize the need for happy and stress-free growing-up years.

don't know well until his course of injections is fully complete. Socialization will help him become well adjusted as he grows up and less prone to being timid or fearful of the new things he will encounter. Your pup's socialization began at the breeder's, but now it is your responsibility to continue it. The socialization he receives up until the age of 12 weeks is the most critical, as this is the time when he forms his impressions of the outside world. The breeder is especially careful during the eight-to-ten-week period, also known as the fear period. The interaction he receives during this time should be gentle and reassuring. Lack of socialization can manifest itself in fear and aggression as the dog grows up. He needs lots of human contact, affection, handling and exposure to other animals.

Once your pup has received his necessary vaccinations, feel free to take him out and about (on his lead, of course). Walk him around the neighborhood, take him on your daily errands, let people pet him, let him meet other dogs and pets, etc. Puppies do not have to try to make friends; there will be no shortage of people who will want to introduce themselves. Just make sure that you carefully supervise each meeting. If the neighborhood children want to say hello, for example, that is great—children and pups most often make great companions. However, sometimes an excited child can unintentionally handle a pup too roughly, or an overzealous pup can playfully nip a little too hard. You want to make socialization experiences positive ones. What a pup learns during this very formative stage will impact his attitude toward future encounters. You want your dog to be comfortable around everyone. A pup that has a bad experience with a child may grow up to be a dog that is shy around or aggressive toward children.

CONSISTENCY IN TRAINING

Dogs, being pack animals, naturally need a leader, or else they try to establish dominance in their packs. When you bring a dog into your family, the choice of who becomes the leader and who becomes the pack is entirely up to you! Your pup's intuitive quest for dominance, coupled with the fact that it is nearly impossible to look at an adorable Havanese pup, with his "puppy-dog" eyes and fuzzy charms, and not cave in, give the pup almost an unfair advantage in getting the upper hand! A pup will definitely test the waters to see what he can and cannot do. Do not give in to those pleading eyes—stand your ground when it comes to disciplining the pup

Havanese destined for the show ring require extensive dog-to-dog socialization. Show dogs encounter each other regularly. Your Havanese must accept other dogs without reservations. This happy Havanese is being shown in Havana.

and make sure that all family members do the same. It will only confuse the pup when Mother tells him to get off the couch when he is used to sitting up there with Father to watch the nightly news. Avoid discrepancies by having all members of the household decide on the rules before the pup even comes home...and be consistent in enforcing them!

PUP MEETS WORLD

Thorough socialization includes not only meeting new people but also being introduced to new experiences such as riding in the car, having his coat brushed, hearing the television, walking in a crowd—the list is endless. The more your pup experiences, and the more positive the experiences are, the less of a shock and the less frightening it will be for your pup to encounter new things.

Early training shapes the dog's personality, so you cannot be unclear in what you expect.

COMMON PUPPY PROBLEMS

The best way to prevent puppy problems is to be proactive in stopping an undesirable behavior as soon as it starts. The old saying "You can't teach an old dog new tricks" does not necessarily hold true, but it *is* true that it is much easier to discourage bad behavior in a young developing pup than to wait until the pup's bad behavior becomes the adult dog's bad habit. There are some problems that are especially prevalent in puppies as they develop.

NIPPING

As puppies start to teethe, they feel the need to sink their teeth into anything available...unfortunately that includes your fingers, arms, hair and toes. You may find this behavior cute for the first five seconds...until you feel just how sharp those puppy teeth are. This is something you want to discourage immediately and consistently with a firm "No!" Then replace your finger with an appropriate chew toy. While this behavior is merely annoying when the dog is young, it can become dangerous if your adult Havanese thinks it is acceptable to nibble on you.

CRYING/WHINING

Your pup will often cry, whine, whimper, howl or make some type of commotion when he is left alone. This is basically his way of calling out for attention to make sure that you know he is there and that you have not forgotten about him. He feels insecure when he is left alone, when you are out of the house and he is in his crate or when you are in another part of the house and he cannot see you. The noise he is making is an expression of the anxiety he feels at being alone, so he needs to be taught that being alone is OK. You are not actually training the dog to stop making noise, you are training him to feel comfortable when he is alone and thus removing the need for him to make the

It is essential for new owners to meet the dam as well as the litter when visiting the breeder. The dam's temperament and behavior will indicate much about her progeny.

noise. This is where the crate with cozy bedding and a toy comes in handy. You want to know that he is safe when you are not there to supervise, and you know that he will be safe in his crate rather than roaming freely about the house. In order for the pup to stay in his crate without making a fuss, he needs to be comfortable in his crate. At the same time, he should not be confined too long in his crate and his area in the house should be expanded as he grows. It is extremely important that the crate is never used as a form of punishment, or the pup will develop a negative association with the crate.

Accustom the pup to the crate in short, gradually increasing time intervals in which you put him in the crate or in a

Two sweet Havanese babies, looking ahead to a bright future.

larger pen, maybe with a treat, and stay in the room with him. If he cries or makes a fuss, do not go to him, but stay in his sight. Gradually he will realize that staying alone is all right, and it will not be so traumatic for him when you are not around. You may want to leave the radio on softly when you leave the house; the sound of human voices may be comforting to him.

CHEWING TIPS

Chewing goes hand in hand with nipping in the sense that a teething puppy is always looking for a way to soothe his aching gums. In this case, instead of chewing on you, he may have taken a liking to your favorite shoe or something else that he should not be chewing. Again, realize that this is a normal canine behavior that does not need to be discouraged, only redirected. Your pup just needs to be taught what is acceptable to chew on and what is off-limits. Consistently tell him "No!" when you catch him chewing on something forbidden and give him a chew toy.

Conversely, praise him when you catch him chewing on something appropriate. In this way, you are discouraging the inappropriate behavior and reinforcing the desired behavior. The puppy's chewing should stop after his adult teeth have come in, but an adult dog continues to chew for various reasons—perhaps because he is bored, needs to relieve tension or just likes to chew. That is why it is important to redirect his chewing when he is still young.

FEEDING CONSIDERATIONS

Originally, the dog was a carnivorous animal, but centuries of domesticity and human company have changed him into an omnivore, which is a good thing. So, along with a portion of meat and proteins of animal origin, vegetables and fruits can be added to his diet to keep him healthy. Avoid sweets and fried foods and, of course, never give your dog small bones. Many commercial dry dog foods contain all the proteins and minerals your dog needs for a complete and healthy diet.

Today the choices of food for your Havanese are many and varied. There are simply dozens of brands of food in all sorts of flavors and textures, ranging from puppy diets to those for seniors. There are even hypoallergenic and low-calorie diets available. Because your Havanese's food has a bearing on coat, health and temperament, it is essential that the most suitable diet is selected for a Havanese of his age. It is fair to say, however, that even dedicated owners can be somewhat perplexed by the enormous range of foods available. Only understanding what is best for your dog will help you reach an informed decision.

Dog foods are produced in three basic types: dry, semi-moist and canned. Dry foods are

STORING DOG FOOD

You must store your dry dog food carefully. Open packages of dog food quickly lose their vitamin value, usually within 90 days of being opened. Mold spores and vermin could also contaminate the food.

useful for the cost-conscious for overall they tend to be less expensive than semi-moist or canned. These contain the least fat and the most preservatives. In general canned foods are made up of 60–70% water, while semi-moist ones often contain so much sugar that they are perhaps the least preferred by owners, even though their dogs seem to like them.

When selecting your dog's

Given the advances of dog food companies today, feeding your Havanese can be fairly simple. Your breeder and vet can recommend a reliable brand of dog food on which to feed your Havanese at all stages of life.

FOOD PREFERENCE

Selecting the best dry dog food is difficult. There is no majority consensus among veterinary scientists as to the value of nutrient analysis (protein, fat, fiber, moisture, ash, cholesterol, minerals, etc.). All agree that feeding trials are what matter most, but you also have to consider the individual dog. The dog's weight, age and activity level, and what pleases his taste, all must be considered. It is probably best to take the advice of your veterinarian. Every dog has individual dietary requirements, and should be fed accordingly.

If your dog is fed a good dry food, he does not require supplements of meat or vegetables. Dogs do appreciate a little variety in their diets, so you may choose to stay with the same brand but vary the flavor. Alternatively, you may wish to add a little flavored stock to give a difference to the taste.

diet, three stages of development must be considered: the puppy stage, adult stage and the senior stage.

PUPPY DIET

Puppies instinctively want to suck milk from their mother's teats and a normal puppy will exhibit this behavior from just a few moments following birth. If puppies do not attempt to suckle within the first half-hour or so, the breeder should encourage them to do so by placing them on the nipples, having selected ones with plenty of milk. This

Puppies nurse from the dam for about the first six weeks. Gradual weaning begins around the third or fourth week by introducing soft solid foods.

FEEDING TIPS

- Dog food must be served at room temperature, neither too hot nor too cold. Fresh water, changed often and served in a clean bowl, is mandatory, especially when feeding dry food.
- Never feed your dog from the table while you are eating, and never feed your dog leftovers from your own meal. They usually contain too much fat and too much seasoning.
- Dogs must chew their food. Hard pellets are excellent; soups and stews are to be avoided.
- Don't add leftovers or any extras to commercial dog food. The normal food is usually balanced, and adding something extra destroys the balance.
- Except for age-related changes, dogs do not require dietary variations. They can be fed the same diet, day after day, without theirbecoming bored or ill.

early milk supply is important in providing colostrum to protect the puppies during the first eight to ten weeks of their lives. Although a mother's milk is much better than any milk formula, despite there being some excellent ones available, if the puppies do not feed, the breeder will have to feed them by hand. For those with less experience, advice from a vet is important so that not only the right quantity of milk is fed but also that of correct quality, fed at suitably frequent intervals, usually every two hours during the first few days of life.

Puppies should be allowed to nurse from their mothers for about the first six weeks, although from the third or fourth week the breeder will begin to introduce small portions of suitable solid food. Most breeders like to introduce alternate milk and meat meals initially, building up to weaning time.

By the time the puppies are seven or a maximum of eight weeks old, they should be fully weaned and fed solely on a proprietary puppy food. Selection of the most suitable, good-quality diet at this time is essential, for a puppy's fastest growth rate is during the first year of life. Vets are usually able to offer advice in this regard. The frequency of meals per day will have to be reduced over time, and when a young Havanese has reached the age of about 12 months, he can be switched to an adult diet.

Puppy and junior diets should be well balanced for the needs of your dog, so that except in certain circumstances additional vitamins, minerals and proteins will not be required.

ADULT DIET
A dog is considered an adult when it has stopped growing, so in general the diet of a Havanese can be changed to an adult one at about 12 months of age. Again you should rely upon your vet or dietary specialist to recommend an acceptable maintenance diet. Major dog food manufacturers specialize in this type of food, and it is just necessary for you to select the one best suited to your dog's needs.

GRAIN-BASED DIETS
Some less expensive dog foods are based on grains and other plant proteins. While these products may appear to be attractively priced, many breeders prefer a diet based on animal proteins and believe that they are more conducive to your dog's health. Many grain-based diets rely on soy protein, which may cause flatulence (passing gas).

There are many cases, however, when your dog might require a special diet. These special requirements should only be recommended by your veterinarian.

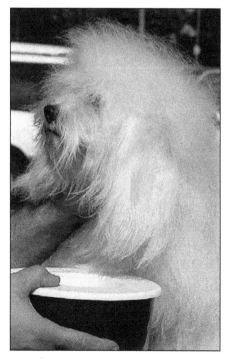

Adult dogs may only require one feeding a day, though some breeders recommend offering two smaller meals.

Active dogs may have different requirements than sedate dogs.

SENIOR DIET

As dogs get older, their metabolism changes. The older dog usually exercises less, moves more slowly and sleeps more. This change in lifestyle and physiological performance requires a change in diet. Since these changes take place slowly, they might not be recognizable. What is easily recognizable is weight gain. By continuing to feed your dog an adult-maintenance diet when he is slowing down metabolically, your dog will gain weight. Obesity in an older dog compounds the health problems that already accompany old age.

As your dog gets older, few of his organs function up to par. The kidneys slow down and the intestines become less efficient. These age-related factors are best handled with a change in diet and a change in feeding schedule to give smaller portions that are more easily digested.

There is no single best diet for every older dog. While many dogs do well on light or senior diets, other dogs do better on puppy diets or special premium diets such as lamb and rice. Be sensitive to your senior Havanese's diet and this will help control other problems that may arise with your old friend.

WATER

Just as your dog needs proper nutrition from his food, water is an essential "nutrient" as well. Water keeps the dog's body properly hydrated and promotes normal function of the body's systems. During housebreaking, it is necessary to keep an eye on how much water your Havanese is drinking, but once he is reliably trained he should have access to clean fresh water at all times. Make sure that the dog's water bowl is clean, and change the water often, making sure that water is always available for your dog, especially if you feed dry food.

EXERCISE

Although a Havanese is small, all dogs require some form of exercise, regardless of size. A sedentary lifestyle is as harmful to a dog as it is to a person. The Havanese is a fairly active breed that enjoys exercise, but you don't have to be an Olympic athlete to provide him with sufficient activity! Regular

A Worthy Investment

Veterinary studies have proven that a balanced high-quality diet pays off in your dog's coat quality, behavior and activity level. Invest in premium brands for the maximum payoff with your dog.

Maintaining the long, silky coat of the Havanese is not as difficult as it looks, and the coat doesn't shed.

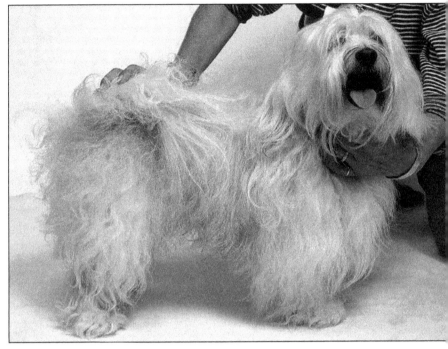

(FACING PAGE) Normal dog hairs enlarged 200 times original size. Inset shows the tip of a growing hair enlarged 1000 times.

walks, play sessions in the yard, or letting the dog run free in the yard under your supervision are sufficient forms of exercise for the Havanese. For those who are more ambitious, you will find that your Havanese also enjoys long walks, an occasional hike or even a swim! Bear in mind that an overweight dog should never be over-exercised suddenly; instead, he should be allowed to increase exercise slowly. Not only is exercise essential to keep the dog's body fit, it is essential to his mental well-being. A bored dog will find something to do, which often manifests itself in some type of destructive behavior. In this sense, it is just as essential for the owner's mental well-being.

GROOMING

BRUSHING

Professional groomers will place the Havanese on a table, leashed for safety, and brush the coat as they fluff it with a blow dryer or a low heat setting. The novice may prefer to use the blow dryer first and brush the coat once it i dry.

If we use the first method, we should use a brush or soft rake. With the second method,

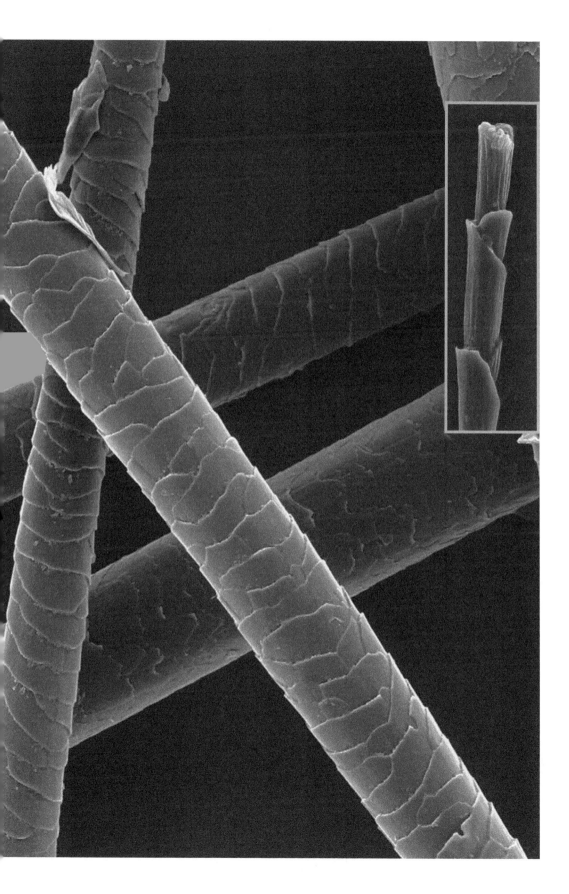

Your local pet shop will have a large supply of grooming tools that you can use on your Havanese.

Do not divide the Havanese's coat in half when combing it. Groom one area at a time, beginning with the comb to ensure that there are no tangles. Then brush over the area.

A small metal comb is useful on the Havanese's muzzle.

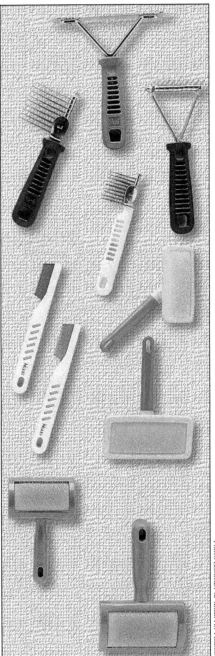

Your local pet shop will have a large supply of grooming tools that you can use on your Havanese.

PHOTO COURTESY OF MIKKI PET PRODUCTS.

we need a metal comb with separated teeth (about eight teeth per inch). In both cases, we should be aware that our dog has to be groomed by layers. That means that the different layers of the coat are raised and groomed separately, beginning with the layer closest to the skin and ending with the top or outer layer, which is what we see. Begin with the legs and the feet, continue with the tail and trunk, working from back to front, then do the chest and neck and, finally, the head. In the muzzle zone, it is preferable to use a smaller metal comb with closer teeth.

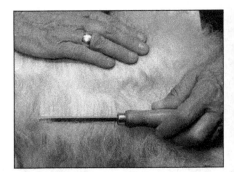

Once the ears have been combed, gently brush over them to give them a natural look.

The beauty of a well-groomed Havanese is that she still looks tousled and carefree! This is Bella, owned by Katy Trevilla of Cuba. The dog should never have the clipped, well-coiffed appearance of a Bichon Frise or Poodle.

GROOMING EQUIPMENT

How much grooming equipment you purchase will depend on how much grooming you are going to do. Here are some basics:

- Natural bristle brush
- Slicker brush
- Metal comb
- Scissors
- Rubber mat
- Dog shampoo
- Spray hose attachment
- Towels
- Blow dryer
- Ear cleaner
- Cotton balls
- Nail clippers
- Dental-care products

You can avoid matting by using this method to groom your dry dog at least twice a week. When you're combing, be careful not to pull out the hair. It's best to work a small area at a time, slowly and patiently, to prevent the undesirable loss of hair. If you occasionally run into a matted layer, we recommend the following treatment:

Avoid cutting the knots. Try to untangle each one with your fingers, pulling the hairs from the center outward. Once the knot is opened with the fingers, you can use a mat-and-tangle comb. This is a special comb that has long, well-spaced teeth with rounded ends to prevent skin injury. In using it, you should always hold the tuft of hair between your fingers close

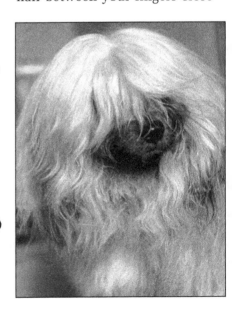

to the skin so that the dog won't be hurt. Also take care to prevent the unnecessary elimination of tufts.

Groom your Havanese in sections, but don't divide the coat in half, as some people do, by creating a part that runs the full length of the back and even up the neck and head. This distorts the image of the dog. Rather, once you've combed an area and are certain the entire layer is untangled, brush the layer lightly and let it fall. The Havanese will shake himself and the hair will fall naturally where it belongs.

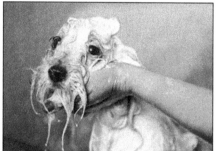

Take great care not to allow soap to irritate the Havanese's eyes. Likewise, a cotton ball in each ear protects them from water entering there.

BATHING

Generally speaking, dogs should be bathed before being groomed. The Havanese that lives in a tropical climate needs to be bathed monthly if his coat is dirty, but one way to keep the dog's coat clean is to give him dry baths with talcum powder. In a cold climate, the Havanese should be bathed less frequently, but his skin must be clean. Remember that every time we bathe a dog, we eliminate from his coat the natural oils that keep him soft and shiny.

Since the coat is a significant factor in the beauty of the Havanese, we should take certain protective measures when we bathe this animal. First of all, if the coat is matted and

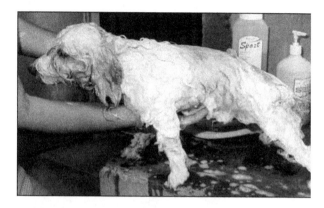

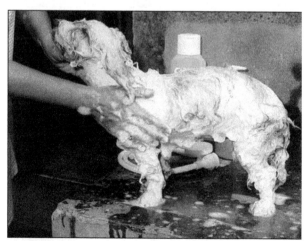

Never bathe an uncombed Havanese! In warmer climates, like Cuba, the Havanese needs to be bathed more frequently than in colder, damper places.

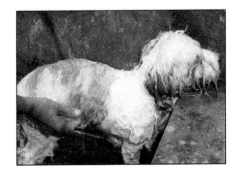

Thoroughly rinse all soap out of the coat. Residue from shampoo can cause irritation to the Havanese's skin. Dry the dog completely, using heavy towels and a blow dryer (on a low setting). Do not hold the blow dryer too close to the dog's coat or you will burn him.

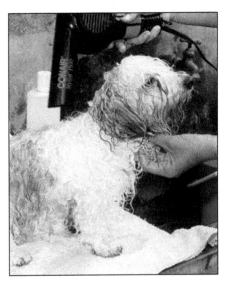

knotted, the tangles should be eliminated before bathing. To facilitate that effort, we can prepare a solution of water and coat conditioner to be sprayed on the coat as we patiently untangle it with a brush or rake, taking care not to pull out the hairs. Only after completely untangling the coat can we bathe the dog. A dog whose coat is properly cared for won't have problems with tangles and can be bathed without any preparation other than a once-over.

In Cuba, dogs are usually bathed in cold water because of the hot climate, though warm water is used in winter. In cold climates, the owner of a Havanese will regulate the

BATHING BEAUTY

Once you are sure that the dog is thoroughly rinsed, squeeze the excess water out of his coat with your hand and dry him with a heavy towel. You can finish the job with a blow dryer on his coat, brushing as you dry. In cold weather, never allow your dog outside with a wet coat.

There are "dry bath" products on the market, which are sprays and powders intended for spot cleaning, that can be used between regular baths if necessary. They are not substitutes for regular baths, but they are easy to use for touch-ups as they do not require rinsing.

SOAP IT UP

The use of human soap products like shampoo, bubble bath and hand soap can be damaging to a dog's coat and skin. Human products are too strong; they remove the protective oils coating the dog's hair and skin that make him water-resistant. Use only shampoo made especially for dogs. You may like to use a medicated shampoo, which will help to keep external parasites at bay.

On warmer days, your Havanese will enjoy bathing in the sun. Remember, these are native tropical dogs who live for sun! Sugar, owned by Barbara Monteagudo.

temperature of the bath to the surroundings, so the water is neither too hot nor too cold.

A coconut aloe vera or a similar shampoo will keep your pet's skin moist. Wet the dog thoroughly and apply shampoo to the trunk, tail, legs, feet and, finally, the head, being careful to keep the ears dry by inserting cotton balls beforehand. Rinse the dog thoroughly, then apply a softener mixed with water. This can be left on the coat to make it softer and more flexible for grooming or it can be rinsed off, at the owner's discretion.

While the Havanese is dripping wet, squeeze the water gently from the tufts and let the animal shake himself thoroughly. Then towel his coat gently to retain the softener, if you decided to leave it on as recommended.

EYE CARE

Sometimes the Havanese tears and, as a result, accumulates dirt below his eyes. When this

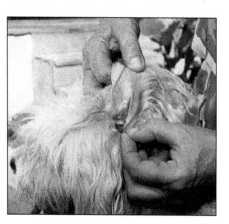

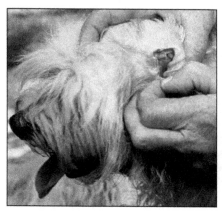

Clean ears are free of odor and secretion. Clean the outer ear gently with a soft wipe, never delving into the ear canal or probing where your cannot see. Remove tufts of hair that grow inside the ear. Be gentle so not to hurt your dog.

If you accustom your Havanese to nail clipping from puppyhood, he should accept the routine as an adult. Most dogs do not like the feeling of nail clipping, so proper introduction and training are key.

happens, rinse the eyes with a saline solution and dry each one with a separate piece of cotton. You can also use a small fine-toothed comb to keep the area clean.

Another method of keeping the face clean is to tie the head hair in a topknot so it doesn't fall over the eyes. This method should be monitored by a professional groomer so the hair isn't pulled or broken, especially if you plan to present your Havanese in a show, for the breed is not permitted to use topknots or any other kind of hair decoration.

EAR CARE

To clean the ears, you should use a blunt-ended tweezers. You can pull out the tufts of hair that grow inside the ears instead of using your fingers. These hairs should be removed carefully, never pulling on large tufts that will hurt your dog. You can then clean the ears with a piece of cotton dipped in an ear-cleaning solution purchased at a pet store. Clean, healthy ears are secretion- and odor-free. Ear problems require veterinary attention.

FOOT AND NAIL CARE

As the Havanese grows and his coat becomes longer, the tufts of hair between the toes also grow, often until they totally cover the cushions of the feet. Our dog becomes uncomfortable as his posture and movement are affected. We need to check the feet systematically and cut out these tufts with small scissors so that the cushions of the feet are completely hair-free.

The nails must also be monitored. A dog's nails should not touch the ground, much less curl into it. Your Havanese may file his nails naturally as he walks on hard surfaces, maintaining them at the proper length. If not, you will have to prevent discomfort and deformation of the feet by cutting the nails—especially the nail of the supplementary toe (dewclaw), if that exists, for it should never touch the ground.

Use a nail trimmer for small dogs or cats, and cut only the protruding part of the nail to avoid hurting the animal. First, raise your dog's foot and hold it against the light to observe what is called the quick, which is the vein that runs through the dog's nail. Do not cut into the quick, or the nail will bleed. If the nails are black, cut a small triangle from the interior to the exterior edge of the nail, no deeper than necessary. Should bleeding occur, press ice on the cut or press your thumb on the affected area until the bleeding stops. You may also apply a styptic powder or pencil.

It's best to accustom your dog to nail cutting and foot care as a pup so that he comes to accept them as a normal part of dog life. Moreover, systematic nail cutting helps the quick contract over time.

ANAL AREA

The anal glands should be systematically discharged to avoid infections and discomfort. It's best to do this while bathing

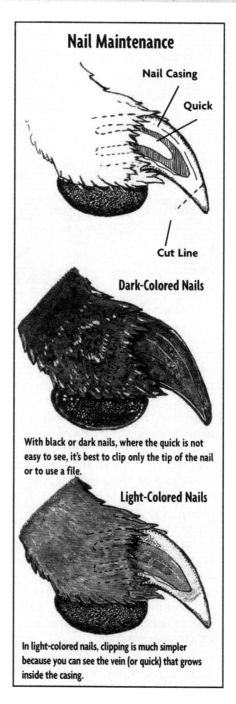

Nail Maintenance

Nail Casing

Quick

Cut Line

Dark-Colored Nails

With black or dark nails, where the quick is not easy to see, it's best to clip only the tip of the nail or to use a file.

Light-Colored Nails

In light-colored nails, clipping is much simpler because you can see the vein (or quick) that grows inside the casing.

You should brush your Havanese's teeth at least once a week with a specially formulated toothpaste for dogs. Human toothpastes are too harsh for your dog's teeth.

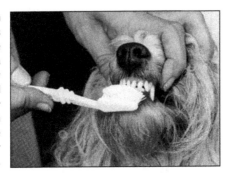

A Havanese whose feet are properly groomed and whose nails are clipped will run with a smooth, easy gait. If your dog exercises frequently on hard surfaces, his nails will wear down naturally and you will not need to clip them as often.

the dog. Just raise the tail and use your thumb and index finger to press the anal area firmly until a dark brown secretion emerges. Wash and rinse the area thoroughly. It is also advisable to trim the hairs on and around the anus so that the area remains free from fecal matter.

TEETH

Removing tufts from your Havanese's feet will help him to stand erect and proud, befitting his noble Cuban heritage.

Once your Havanese has his permanent teeth, we should take measures to keep the mouth free of tartar buildup and other accumulations. It's a good idea to accustom the pup to having his teeth brushed weekly with a toothpaste for dogs. By the time it reaches adulthood, he will tolerate this kind of cleaning without objection.

Gnawing on bones, which should always be large, hard beef bones that can't be splintered or swallowed, is a natural way for dogs to clean their teeth. Pet stores also carry commercial products designed for this purpose, the most reliable of which are made of durable nylon.

If you notice that your dog's breath smells bad or his teeth have an accumulation of tartar, consult the veterinarian or a grooming professional about how best to eliminate these residues without harming the animal.

POSTURE

Although posture may seem somewhat unrelated to the topic of grooming, we've decided to refer to it in this chapter to help improve the proper overall image of your Havanese. By following the advice on nail cutting and tuft removal, you will help your dog's posture. And if you want to do a bit more for your pet, we can also recommend that you make a habit of elevating his food above floor level. The ideal is to locate the food at the dog's head height so the dog need not assume an uncomfortable posture to eat. If you begin doing this from the time he's a pup, raising the plate level according to his growth, you will note an improvement in neck posture.

Another recourse is to stroke your dog on the underside of the neck rather than on top of the head when he comes to you. In the first place, it's more pleasing for him and, in the second place, you're training him to walk with his head up, for he will quickly learn that's when his master caresses him.

TRAVELING WITH YOUR DOG

CAR TRAVEL

You should accustom your Havanese to riding in a car at an early age. You may or may not take him in the car often, but at

The most acceptable, safest way of traveling with your Havanese in a car is in a crate. It is dangerous for the dog to have free access to all parts of the vehicle while it is moving.

the very least he will need to go to the vet and you do not want these trips to be traumatic for the dog or a big hassle for you. The safest way for a dog to ride in the car is in his crate. If he uses a crate in the house, you can use the same crate for travel.

Put the pup in the crate and see how he reacts. If he seems uneasy, you can have a passenger hold him on his lap while you drive. Another option is a specially made safety harness for dogs, which straps the dog in much like a seat belt. Do not let the dog roam loose in the vehicle—this is very dangerous! If you should stop short, your dog

ON THE ROAD
If you are going on a long car trip with your dog, be sure the hotels are dog-friendly. Many hotels do not accept dogs. Also take along some water or some ice that can be thawed and offered to your dog if he becomes overheated. Most dogs like to lick ice.

Traveling in the basket of a morotcycle is not an acceptable mode of transport for the Havanese, but it sure makes a great photograph!

TRAVEL TIP

Never leave your dog alone in the car. In hot weather, your dog can die from the high temperature inside a closed vehicle; even a car parked in the shade can heat up very quickly. Leaving the window open is dangerous as well since the dog can hurt himself trying to get out.

can be thrown and injured. If the dog starts climbing on you and pestering you while you are driving, you will not be able to concentrate on the road. It is an unsafe situation for everyone—human and canine.

For long trips, be prepared to stop to let the dog relieve himself. Bring along whatever you need to clean up after him. You should take along some paper towels and perhaps some old rags for use should he have an accident in the car or suffer from motion sickness.

AIR TRAVEL

Contact your chosen airline before proceeding with travel plans that include your Havanese. The dog will be required to travel in a fiberglass crate and you should always check in advance with the airline regarding specific requirements for the crate's size, type and labeling. To help put the dog at ease, give him one of his favorite toys in the crate. Do not feed the dog for several hours prior to checking in so that you minimize his need to relieve himself. Some airlines require you to provide documentation as to when the dog has last been fed. In any case, a light meal is best. For long trips, you will have to attach food and water bowls to the dog's crate so that airline employees can tend to him between legs of the trip.

Check to see if your Havanese

qualifies as a "carry-on." If not, he will travel in a different area than the human passengers. Regardless, make sure your dog is properly identified and that your contact information appears on his ID tags and on his crate. Every rule must be strictly followed to prevent the risk of getting separated from your dog.

VACATIONS AND BOARDING
So you want to take a family vacation—and you want to include *all* members of the family. You would probably make arrangements for accommodations ahead of time anyway, but this is especially important when traveling with a dog. You do not want to make an overnight stop at the only place around for miles and find out that they do not allow dogs. Also, you do not want to reserve a place for your family without confirming that you are traveling with a dog because, if it is against the hotel's policy, you may not have a place to stay.

Alternatively, if you are traveling and choose not to bring your Havanese, you will have to make arrangements for him while you are away. Some options are to take him to a

Havanese are willing passengers and look forward to a Sunday drive. Be sure that your dogs are secured properly in your car before driving. You might consider a doggie harness that attaches to the car's seat belts if you'd rather not use a crate. Sugar and Ambar, owned by Barbara Monteagudo.

Should you find it necessary to board your Havanese while you are on vacation, locate a facility with clean accommodations and a friendly staff.

friend's house to stay while you are gone, to have a trusted friend stop by often or stay at your house or to bring your dog to a reputable boarding kennel. If you choose to board him at a kennel, you should visit in advance to see the facility, how clean they are and where the dogs are kept. Talk to some of the employees and see how they treat the dogs—do they spend time with the dogs, play with them, groom them, etc.? Also find out the kennel's policy on vaccinations and what they

COLLAR REQUIRED

If your dog gets lost, he is not able to ask for directions home. Identification tags fastened to the collar give important information—the dog's name, the owner's name, the owner's address and a telephone number where the owner can be reached. This makes it easy for whomever finds the dog to contact the owner and arrange to have the dog returned. An added advantage is that a person will be more likely to approach a lost dog who has ID tags on his collar; it tells the person that this is somebody's pet rather than a stray. This is the easiest and fastest method of identification, provided that the tags stay on the collar and the collar stays on the dog.

IDENTIFICATION OPTIONS

As puppies become more and more expensive, especially those puppies of high quality for showing and/or breeding, they have a greater chance of being stolen. The usual collar dog tag is, of course, easily removed. But there are two more permanent techniques that have become widely used for identification.

The puppy microchip implantation involves the injection of a small microchip, about the size of a corn kernel, under the skin of the dog. If your dog shows up at a clinic or shelter, or is offered for resale under less-than-savory circumstances, it can be positively identified by the microchip. The microchip is scanned, and a registry quickly identifies you as the owner.

Tattooing is done on various parts of the dog, from his belly to his ears. The number tattooed can be your telephone number, your dog's registration number or any other number that you can easily memorize. When professional dog thieves see a tattooed dog, they usually lose interest. For the safety of our dogs, no laboratory facility or dog broker will accept a tattooed dog as stock.

Discuss microchipping and tattooing with your veterinarian and breeder. Some vets perform these services on their own premises for a reasonable fee. To ensure that your dog's identification is effective, be certain that the dog is then properly registered with a legitimate national database.

Your Havanese's ID tags should be securely attached to his collar.

require. This is for all of the dogs' safety, since when dogs are kept together, there is a greater risk of diseases being passed from dog to dog.

IDENTIFICATION

Your Havanese is your valued companion and friend. That is why you always keep a close eye on him and you have made sure that he cannot escape from the yard or wriggle out of his collar and run away from you. However, accidents can happen and there may come a time when your dog unexpectedly gets separated from you. If this unfortunate event should occur, the first thing on your mind will be finding him. Proper identification, including an ID tag and possibly a tattoo and/or a microchip, will increase the chances of his being returned to you safely and quickly.

The Havanese is the favorite pet in Cuba. This one is at home on the farm in front of Cuba's other famous export, tobacco. The barn in the background is where the tobacco is dried.

TRAINING YOUR
HAVANESE

Puppies learn from their mother in a natural way. But when you bring a Havanese into your house, you want to teach him habits and customs appropriate to your family life. Indeed you also want to give him some basic obedience training so he can walk correctly on leash, and come or sit on command.

Basic training will be useful for your Havanese and also for you. As we noted earlier, the dog is a pack animal, programmed by nature to lead or to follow. When a dog enters a human pack, his role is to *follow*. Under all circumstances, the one he follows has to be

REAP THE REWARDS
If you start with a normal, healthy dog and give him time, patience and some carefully executed lessons, you will reap the rewards of that training for the life of the dog. And what a life it will be! The two of you will find immeasurable pleasure in the companionship you have built together with love, respect and understanding.

you. As the leader, you give your dog a feeling of security and protection, and the guidance he needs. A dog left to his own devices is not a balanced or happy animal.

A Havanese's education begins the very instant you bring him home. At first, your pup should be confined to his own area. To avoid accidents and destructive behavior, an animal should be housebroken before he is given the run of your home. Teach your Havanese by habit, never by hitting, that he has a fixed place to eat, a fixed place to urinate and defecate and a fixed place to sleep.

It is also important to teach your dog to respond to his name. Call him by name to feed him or pet him, but never call him by name when you're going to scold him. For that, there's just one word, spoken firmly and definitively: No!

You should recognize that the puppy will do everything possible to control you, which you cannot permit. You have to impose your will, little by little, not by force, but by making him understand. To make a dog understand us, we must learn to put ourselves in his place and not presume—as many people do—that the dog is human and lives in our world. That is impossible. The essential qualities for teaching are patience and perseverance. Repeat the command until the dog understands what is expected of him.

In giving commands, we should use short, clear words that are always the same. For example, when we call the dog, we can't alternate between "Come" and "Here." Choose one and keep it so you won't confuse him. Also, speak, don't scream, your commands.

Personal experience has taught me that one factor in the man-dog relationship that most owners neglect, even though it is of primary importance and utility, is talking to your dog. Verbal communication is an excellent method of directing

your dog with the guarantee that you will always be obeyed. But you have to know how. The first thing to do is relax and pay no attention to what others might think of you. (I know men who don't like to sweet-talk their dogs because they consider it unmasculine.) Talk to your dog about everything that affects him. If you're going to give him medicine, first talk to him softly and lovingly to calm him. The same thing if you're going to groom him. Show him the comb,

A well-trained Havanese is a joy to his owner. This is Cuban champion Esmerelda de la Giraldilla, owned by Merita Batista and Annia Barroso, in front of La Chorrera Castle in Havana.

PARENTAL GUIDANCE

Training a dog is a life experience. Many parents admit that much of what they know about raising children they learned from caring for their dogs. Dogs respond to love, fairness and guidance, just as children do. Become a good dog owner and you may become an even better parent.

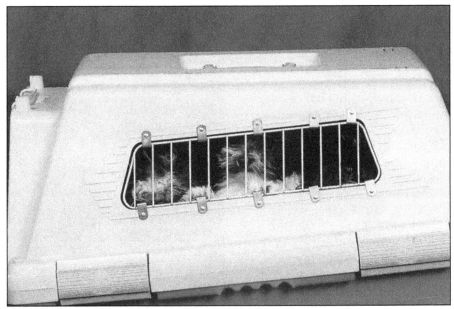

let him smell it, tell him it won't hurt...and you'll see the results.

In many cases, we humans act as if the dog were not a living creature with concerns and fears. We think we have the right to do what we want with him: check his body, poke into his ears or—without any preamble—start clipping his nails or stick a needle in his skin to vaccinate him. Put yourself in your dog's place and imagine if someone treated you that way. Wouldn't you feel violated? How much better it would be if you were first told in detail what to expect. Well, the same is true of your dog. We should talk to him softly, with love, so

he understands us and our intentions. Of course, he won't understand the words, but he will understand our tone of voice and will respond with confidence and tranquility. This confidence is just what we need

MEALTIME

Mealtime should be a peaceful time for your puppy. Do not put his food and water bowls in a high-traffic area in the house. For example, give him his own little corner of the kitchen where he can eat undisturbed and where he will not be underfoot. Do not allow small children or other family members to disturb the pup when he is eating.

THINK BEFORE YOU BARK
Dogs are sensitive to their masters'
moods and emotions. Use your voice
wisely when communicating with your
dog. Never raise your voice at your
dog unless you are trying to correct
him. "Barking" at your dog can
become as meaningless as "dogspeak"
is to you.

to be able to direct him easily,
without verbal or physical
aggression. Try it, and when you
become accustomed to this
method, perhaps you'll agree
with me that most of us operate
on the absurd pretext of being
understood without offering
explanations, and this is as true
in human relations as in relations with your animals.

The most appropriate age to
start basic training is three
months, before the dog acquires
bad habits. Our goal is to have
our Havanese obey us cheer-
fully, with the express desire of
pleasing us, and not out of fear.

You may want to look into
the training courses available in
many books and at obedience
schools that offer such instruction. Whatever method you
choose to follow, we can only
add that a good teacher should
know when to reward and when
to punish. Punishment does not
mean hitting the dog, but rather

reprimanding him with a firm
"No" when he does something
improper. A reward should be
given to reinforce *any* positive
conduct: each time your
Havanese does something right,
caress him and praise him.
Better than any food treat, the
best reward a dog can have is
his master's love and approval.

HOUSEBREAKING
You can train a puppy to relieve
himself wherever you choose,
but this must be somewhere
suitable. You should bear in
mind from the outset that when

Teach your
Havanese the rules
of your household
from puppyhood.
You cannot allow
your dog to sit on
the furniture
outdoors and then
forbid him to sit
on the furniture
inside your home.

If you acclimate your Havanese to relieving himself on grass, this is the surface that he will always seek out. Grass is the most common choice since it is available most anywhere you go.

your puppy is old enough to go out in public places, any canine deposits must be removed at once. You will always have to carry with you a small plastic bag or "poop-scoop."

Outdoor training includes such surfaces as grass, dirt and cement. Indoor training usually means training your dog to newspaper. When deciding on the surface and location that you will want your Havanese to use, be sure it is going to be permanent. Training your dog to grass and then changing your mind two months later is extremely difficult for both dog and owner.

Next, choose the command you will use each and every time you want your puppy to relieve himself. "Go hurry up" and "Potty" are examples of commands commonly used by dog owners. Get in the habit of

giving the puppy your chosen relief command before you take him out. That way, when he becomes an adult, you will be able to determine if he wants to go out when you ask him. A confirmation will be signs of interest, such as wagging his tail, watching you intently, going to the door, etc.

PUPPY'S NEEDS
Your puppy needs to relieve himself after play periods, after each meal, after he has been sleeping and any time he indicates that he is looking for a place to urinate or defecate. The urinary and intestinal tract muscles of very young puppies are not fully developed. Therefore, like human babies, puppies need to relieve themselves frequently.

CALM DOWN
Dogs will do anything for your attention. If you reward the dog when he is calm and attentive, you will develop a well-mannered dog. If, on the other hand, you greet your dog excitedly and encourage him to wrestle with you, the dog will greet you the same way and you will have a hyperactive dog on your hands.

CANINE DEVELOPMENT SCHEDULE

It is important to understand how and at what age a puppy develops into adulthood.
If you are a puppy owner, consult the following Canine Development Schedule to
determine the stage of development your puppy is currently experiencing.
This knowledge will help you as you work with the puppy in the weeks and months ahead.

Period	Age	Characteristics
FIRST TO THIRD	BIRTH TO SEVEN WEEKS	Puppy needs food, sleep and warmth, and responds to simple and gentle touching. Needs mother for security and disciplining. Needs littermates for learning and interacting with other dogs. Pup learns to function within a pack and learns pack order of dominance. Begin socializing pup with adults and children for short periods. Pup begins to become aware of his environment.
FOURTH	EIGHT TO TWELVE WEEKS	Brain is fully developed. Needs socializing with outside world. Remove from mother and littermates. Needs to change from canine pack to human pack. Human dominance necessary. Fear period occurs between 8 and 12 weeks. Avoid fright and pain.
FIFTH	THIRTEEN TO SIXTEEN WEEKS	Training and formal obedience should begin. Less association with other dogs, more with people, places, situations. Period will pass easily if you remember this is pup's change-to-adolescence time. Be firm and fair. Flight instinct prominent. Permissiveness and over-disciplining can do permanent damage. Praise for good behavior.
JUVENILE	FOUR TO EIGHT MONTHS	Another fear period about 7 to 8 months of age. It passes quickly, but be cautious of fright and pain. Sexual maturity reached. Dominant traits established. Dog should understand sit, down, come and stay by now.

NOTE: THESE ARE APPROXIMATE TIME FRAMES. ALLOW FOR INDIVIDUAL DIFFERENCES IN PUPPIES.

HOW MANY TIMES A DAY?

AGE	RELIEF TRIPS
To 14 weeks	10
14–22 weeks	8
22–32 weeks	6
Adulthood	4
(dog stops growing)	

These are estimates, of course, but they are a guide to the *minimum* number of opportunities a dog should have each day to relieve himself.

Take your puppy out often—every hour for a ten-week-old, for example, and always immediately after sleeping and eating. The older the puppy, the less often he will need to relieve himself. Finally, as a mature healthy adult, he will require only three to five relief trips per day.

HOUSING

Since the types of housing and control you provide for your puppy has a direct relationship on the success of house-training, we consider the various aspects of both before we begin training.

Bringing a new puppy home and turning him loose in your house can be compared to turning a child loose in a sports arena and telling the child that the place is all his! The sheer enormity of the place would be too much for him to handle.

Instead, offer the puppy clearly defined areas where he can play, sleep, eat and live. A room of the house where the family gathers is the most obvious choice. Puppies are social animals and need to feel a part of the pack right from the start. Hearing your voice, watching you while you are doing things and smelling you nearby are all positive reinforcers that he is now a member of your pack. Usually a family room, the kitchen or a nearby adjoining breakfast area is ideal for providing safety and security for both puppy and owner.

Within that room, there should be a smaller area which the puppy can call his own. An alcove, a wire or fiberglass dog crate or a partitioned (not boarded!) corner from which he can view the activities of his new family will be fine. Dogs are, by nature, clean animals and will not remain close to their relief areas unless forced to do so. In those cases, they then become dirty dogs and usually remain that way for life.

The designated area should contain clean bedding and a toy. Water must always be available, in a non-spill container, although you should avoid putting food and water in the dog's crate until he is reliably housebroken.

CONTROL

By *control*, we mean helping the puppy to create a lifestyle pattern that will be compatible to that of his human pack (*you*!). Just as we guide little children to learn our way of life, we must show the puppy when it is time to play, eat, sleep, exercise and even entertain himself.

Your puppy should always sleep in a designated space. He should also learn that, during times of household confusion and excessive human activity such as at breakfast when family members are preparing for the day, he can play by himself in relative safety and comfort in his designated area. Each time you leave the puppy alone, he should understand exactly where he is to stay. You can

A wire crate offers your Havanese many advantages. In warmer climate, the wire crate is ideal for ventilation.

gradually increase the time he is left alone to get him used to it.

Puppies are chewers. They cannot tell the difference between lamp cords, television wires, shoes, table legs, etc. Chewing into a television wire, for example, can be fatal to the puppy, while a shorted wire can start a fire in the house.

If the puppy chews on the arm of the chair when he is alone, you will probably discipline him angrily when you get

If convenient or desirable, section off a part of your patio where your Havanese can enjoy some time outdoors.

Attentive and eager to please, the Havanese makes an easily trained companion.

home. Thus, he makes the association that your coming home means he is going to be punished. (He will not remember chewing the chair and is incapable of making the association of the discipline with his naughty deed.) Crating the puppy avoids his engaging in dangerous and/or destructive behavior when you're not there to supervise.

Times of excitement, such as visits, family parties, etc., can be fun for the puppy, providing he can view the activities from the security of his designated area. He is not underfoot and he is not being fed all sorts of tidbits that will probably cause him stomach distress, yet he still feels a part of the fun.

SCHEDULE

A puppy should be taken to his relief area each time he is released from his designated area, after meals, after play sessions, when he first awakens in the morning (at age ten weeks, this can mean 5 a.m.!). The puppy will indicate that he's ready "to go" by circling or sniffing busily—do not misinterpret these signs. For a puppy around ten weeks of age, a routine of taking him out every hour is necessary. As the puppy grows, he will be able to wait for longer periods of time.

Keep trips to his relief area short. Stay no more than five or six minutes and then return to the house. If he goes during that time, praise him lavishly and take him indoors immediately. If he does not, but he has an acci-

PAPER CAPER

Never line your pup's sleeping area with newspaper. Puppy litters are usually raised on newspaper and, once in your home, the puppy will immediately associate newspaper with voiding. Never put newspaper on any floor while house-training, as this will only confuse the puppy. If you are paper-training him, use paper in his designated relief area only. Finally, restrict water intake after evening meals. Offer a few licks at a time—never let a young puppy gulp water after meals.

THE CLEAN LIFE

By providing sleeping and resting quarters that fit the dog, and offering frequent opportunities to relieve himself outside his quarters, the puppy quickly learns that the outdoors (or the newspaper if you are training him to paper) is the place to go when he needs to urinate or defecate. It also reinforces his innate desire to keep his sleeping quarters clean. This, in turn, helps develop the muscle control that will eventually produce a dog with clean living habits.

dent when you go back indoors, pick him up immediately, say "No! No!" and return to his relief area. Wait a few minutes, then return to the house again. Never hit a puppy or put his face in urine or excrement when he has an accident!

Once indoors, put the puppy in his crate until you have had time to clean up his accident. Then release him to the family area and watch him more closely than before. Chances are, his accident was a result of your not picking up his signal or waiting too long before offering him the opportunity to relieve himself. Never hold a grudge against the puppy for accidents.

Let the puppy learn that going outdoors means it is time to relieve himself, not play. Once trained, he will be able to play indoors and out and still differentiate between the times for play versus the times for relief.

Help him develop regular hours for naps, being alone, playing by himself and just resting, all in his crate. Encourage him to entertain himself while you are busy with your activities. Let him learn that having you near is comforting, but it is not your main purpose in life to provide him with undivided attention.

Each time you put your puppy in his own area, use the same command, whatever suits best. Soon, he will run to his crate or special area when he hears you say those words.

Crate training provides safety for you, the puppy and the home. It also provides the puppy with a feeling of security, and that helps the puppy achieve self-confidence and clean habits. Remember that one of the primary ingredients in house-training your puppy is control. Regardless of your lifestyle, there will always be

Be an ideal dog owner: clean up after your dog whether in a public place or in your own yard.

occasions when you will need to have a place where your dog can stay and be happy and safe. Crate training is the answer for now and in the future.

In conclusion, a few key elements are really all you need for a successful house-training method—consistency, frequency, praise, control and supervision. By following these procedures with a normal, healthy puppy, you and the puppy will soon be past the stage of accidents and ready to move on to a clean and rewarding life together.

THE SUCCESS METHOD

Success that comes by luck is usually short-lived. Success that comes by well-thought-out proven methods is often more easily achieved and permanent. This is the Success Method. It is designed to give you, the puppy owner, a simple yet proven way to help your puppy develop clean living habits and a feeling of security in his new environment.

6 Steps to Successful Crate Training

1 Tell the puppy "Crate time!" and place him in the crate with a small treat (a piece of cheese or half of a biscuit). Let him stay in the crate for five minutes while you are in the same room. Then release him and praise lavishly. Never release him when he is fussing. Wait until he is quiet before you let him out.

2 Repeat Step 1 several times a day.

3 The next day, place the puppy in the crate as before. Let him stay there for ten minutes. Do this several times.

4 Continue building time in five-minute increments until the puppy stays in his crate for 30 minutes with you in the room. Always take him to his relief area after prolonged periods in his crate.

5 Now go back to Step 1 and let the puppy stay in his crate for five minutes, this time while you are out of the room.

6 Once again, build crate time in five-minute increments with you out of the room. When the puppy will stay willingly in his crate (he may even fall asleep!) for 30 minutes with you out of the room, he will be ready to stay in it for several hours at a time.

An impressionable, young Havanese puppy will rely on you for all his needs. This includes his instruction. If you are confused about how to house-train your dog, imagine how he must feel!

ROLES OF DISCIPLINE, REWARD AND PUNISHMENT

Discipline, training one to act in accordance with rules, brings order to life. It is as simple as that. Without discipline, partic-

ularly in a group society, chaos reigns supreme and the group will eventually perish. Humans and canines are social animals and need some form of discipline in order to function effectively. They must procure food, reproduce to keep the species going and protect their home base and their young.

If there were no discipline in the lives of social animals, they would eventually die from starvation and/or predation by other stronger animals. In the case of domestic canines, dogs need discipline in their lives in order to understand how their pack (you and other family members) functions and how they must act in order to survive.

A large humane society in a highly populated area recently surveyed dog owners regarding their satisfaction with their relationships with their dogs.

Your Havanese will do his best to express his desires: "I want to go out now!"

People who had trained their dogs were 75% more satisfied with their pets than those who had never trained their dogs.

Dr. Edward Thorndike, a noted psychologist, established *Thorndike's Theory of Learning*, which states that a behavior that results in a pleasant event tends to be repeated. Likewise, a behavior that results in an unpleasant event tends not to be repeated. It is this theory on which training methods are based today. For example, if you manipulate a dog to perform a specific behavior and reward him for doing it, he is likely to do it again because he enjoyed the end result.

Occasionally, punishment, a penalty inflicted for an offense, is necessary. The best type of punishment often comes from an outside source. For example, a child is told not to touch the stove because he may get burned. He disobeys and touches the stove. In doing so, he receives a burn. From that time on, he respects the heat of the stove and avoids contact with it. Therefore, a behavior that results in an unpleasant event tends not to be repeated.

A good example of a dog learning the hard way is the dog who chases the house cat. He is told many times to leave the cat alone, yet he persists in teasing the cat. Then, one day he begins chasing the cat but the cat turns and swipes a claw across the dog's face, leaving him with a painful gash on his nose. The final result is that the dog stops chasing the cat.

TRAINING EQUIPMENT

COLLAR AND LEAD

For a Havanese, the collar and leash that you use for training must be one with which you are easily able to work, not too heavy for the dog and perfectly safe. For the Havanese, a light nylon leash and collar is perfectly suitable.

TREATS

Assuming that your Havanese is performing on command primarily to please you, his owner, you may wish to incorporate food

PLAN TO PLAY

The puppy should also have regular play and exercise sessions when he is with you or a family member. Exercise for a very young puppy can consist of a short walk around the house or yard. Playing can include fetching games with a large ball or a special toy. (All puppies teethe and need soft things upon which to chew.) Remember to restrict play periods to indoors within his living area (the family room, for example) until he is completely house-trained.

The Havanese is a naturally beautiful dog with a temperament to match. With your guidance, he will become a companion beyond compare.

Do not attempt to train your dog in an area where there are many distractions—even if the distractions are as tiny as a flea!

rewards into your training routine. Have a bag of treats on hand. Something nutritious and easy to swallow works best. Use a soft treat, a chunk of cheese or a piece of cooked chicken rather than a dry biscuit. By the time the dog gets done chewing a dry treat, he will forget why he is being rewarded in the first place! Using food rewards will not teach a dog to beg at the table—the only way to teach a dog to beg at the table is to give him food from the table. In training, rewarding the dog with a food treat will help him associate praise and the treats with learning new behaviors that obviously please his owner.

(FACING PAGE) While your Havanese should obey your commands out of love and respect for you, many trainers rely upon food treats to "bribe" the dog to pay attention. Use treats wisely—or you will not be in control, the cheese will!

LANGUAGE BARRIER

Dogs do not understand our language and have to rely on tone of voice more than just words or sound. They can be trained to react to a certain sound, at a certain volume. If you say "No, Oliver" in a very soft, pleasant voice, it will not have the same meaning as "No, Oliver!!" when you raise your voice.

You should never use the dog's name during a reprimand, just the command "No! " You never want the dog to associate his name with a negative experience or reprimand.

TRAINING BEGINS: ASK THE DOG A QUESTION

In order to teach your dog anything, you must first get his attention. After all, he cannot learn anything if he is looking away from you with his mind on something else.

To get his attention, ask him "School?" and immediately walk over to him and give him a treat as you tell him "Good dog." Wait a minute or two and repeat the routine, this time with a treat in your hand as you approach within a foot of the dog. Do not go directly to him, but stop about a foot short of him and hold out the treat as you ask "School?" He will see you approaching with a treat in your hand and most likely begin walking toward you. As you meet, give him the treat and praise again.

The third time, ask the question, have a treat in your hand and walk only a short distance

Reward your dog with petting and praise when he has obeyed your command. Your affection and approval are the best rewards you can give.

toward the dog so that he must walk almost all the way to you. As he reaches you, give him the treat and praise again.

By this time, the dog will probably be getting the idea that if he pays attention to you, especially when you ask that question, it will pay off in treats and fun activities for him. In other words, he learns that "school" means doing fun things with you that result in treats and positive attention for him.

Remember that the dog does not understand your verbal language, he only recognizes sounds. Your question translates to a series of sounds for him, and those sounds become the signal to go to you and pay attention; if he does, he will get to interact with you plus receive treats and praise.

THE BASIC COMMANDS

TEACHING SIT

Now that you have the dog's attention, attach his lead and hold it in your left hand and a food treat in your right. Place your food hand at the dog's nose and let him lick the treat but not take it from you. Say "Sit" and slowly raise your food hand from in front of the dog's nose up over his head so that he is looking at the ceiling. As he bends his head upward, he will have to bend his knees to maintain his balance. As he bends his knees, he will assume a sit position. At that point, release the food treat and praise lavishly with comments such as

FETCH!

Play fetching games with your puppy in an enclosed area where he can retrieve his toy and bring it back to you. Always use a toy or object designated just for this purpose. Never use a shoe, sock or other item he may later confuse with those in your closet or underneath your chair.

"Good dog! Good sit!" Remember to always praise enthusiastically, because dogs relish verbal praise from their owners and feel so proud of themselves whenever they accomplish a behavior.

You will not use food forever in getting the dog to obey your commands. Food is only used to teach new behaviors, and once the dog knows what you want when you give a specific command, you will wean him off the food treats but still maintain the verbal praise. After all, you will always have your voice with you, and there will be many times when you have no food rewards but expect the dog to obey.

TEACHING DOWN

Teaching the down exercise is easy when you understand how the dog perceives the down position, and it is very difficult when you do not. Dogs perceive the down position as a submis-

sive one; therefore, teaching the down exercise using a forceful method can sometimes make the dog develop such a fear of the down that he either runs away when you say "Down" or he attempts to snap at the person who tries to force him down.

Have the dog sit close alongside your left leg, facing in the same direction as you are. Hold

Use food to teach new commands. Once the dog associates the word with the desired response, food should not be the key motivating factor.

The sit/stay exercise develops from the proper execution of the sit command. Remember to use food treats sparingly so that the dog doesn't confuse lesson time with meal time!

the lead in your left hand and a food treat in your right. Now place your left hand lightly on the top of the dog's shoulders where they meet above the spinal cord. Do not push down on the dog's shoulders; simply rest your left hand there so you can guide the dog to lie down close to your left leg rather than to swing away from your side when he drops.

Now place the food hand at the dog's nose, say "Down" very softly (almost a whisper) and slowly lower the food hand to the dog's front feet. When the food hand reaches the floor, begin moving it forward along the floor in front of the dog. Keep talking softly to the dog, saying things like, "Do you want this treat? You can do this, good dog." Your reassuring tone of voice will help calm the dog as he tries to follow the food hand in order to get the treat.

When the dog's elbows touch the floor, release the food and praise softly. Try to get the dog to maintain that down position for several seconds before you let him sit up again. The goal here is to get the dog to settle down and not feel threatened in the down position.

TEACHING STAY

It is easy to teach the dog to stay in either a sit or a down position. Again, we use food and praise during the teaching process as we help the dog to

PRACTICE MAKES PERFECT!

• Have training lessons with your dog every day in several short segments—three to five times a day for a few minutes at a time is ideal.

• Do not have long practice sessions. The dog will become easily bored.

• Never practice when you are tired, ill, worried or in an otherwise negative mood. This will transmit to the dog and may have an adverse effect on his performance.

• Think fun, short and above all *positive!* End each session on a high note, rather than a failed exercise, and make sure to give a lot of praise. Enjoy the training and help your dog enjoy it, too.

understand exactly what it is that we are expecting him to do.

To teach the sit/stay, start with the dog sitting on your left side as before and hold the lead in your left hand. Have a food treat in your right hand and place your food hand at the dog's nose. Say "Stay" and step out on your right foot to stand directly in front of the dog, toe to toe, as he licks and nibbles the treat. Be sure to keep his head facing upward to maintain the sit position. Count to five and then swing around to stand next to the dog again with him on your left. As soon as you get back to the original position, release the food and praise lavishly.

To teach the down/stay, do the down as previously described. As soon as the dog lies down, say "Stay" and step out on your right foot just as you did in the sit/stay. Count to five and then return to stand beside the dog with him on your left side. Release the treat and praise as always.

Within a week or ten days, you can begin to add a bit of distance between you and your dog when you leave him. When you do, use your left hand open with the palm facing the dog as a stay signal, much the same as the hand signal a police officer uses to stop traffic at an intersection. Hold the food treat in your right hand as before, but this time the food is not touching the dog's nose. He will watch the food hand and quickly learn that he is going to get that treat as soon as you return to his side.

Speak clearly and confidently in commanding your Havanese. Do not shout or adopt a dictator-like tone. Your Havanese is a sensitive and intelligent dog that responds best to a gentle and fair trainer.

When you can stand 3 feet away from your dog for 30 seconds, you can then begin building time and distance in both stays. Eventually, the dog can be expected to remain in the stay position for prolonged periods of time until you return to him or call him to you. Always praise lavishly when he stays.

TEACHING COME

If you make teaching "come" a fun experience, you should never have a student that does not love the game or that fails to come when called. The secret, it seems, is never to teach the word "come."

At times when an owner most wants his dog to come when called, the owner is likely upset or anxious and he allows these feelings to come through in the tone of his voice when he calls his dog.

"COME" ... BACK

Never call your dog to come to you for a correction or scold him when he reaches you. That is the quickest way to turn a come command into "Go away fast!" Dogs think only in the present tense, and your dog will connect the scolding with coming to you, not with the misbehavior of a few moments earlier.

Hearing that desperation in his owner's voice, the dog fears the results of going to him and therefore either disobeys outright or runs in the opposite direction. The secret, therefore, is to teach the dog a game and, when you want him to come to you, simply play the game. It is practically a no-fail solution!

To begin, have several members of your family take a few food treats and each go into a different room in the house. Take turns calling the dog, and each person should celebrate the dog's finding him with a treat and lots of happy praise. When a person calls the dog, he is actually inviting the dog to find him and get a treat as a reward for "winning."

A few turns of the "Where are you?" game and the dog will figure out that everyone is playing the game and that each person has a big celebration awaiting his success at locating them. Once he learns to love the game, simply calling out "Where are you?" will bring him running from wherever he is when he hears that all-important question.

The come command is recognized as one of the most important things to teach a dog, but there are trainers who work with thousands of dogs and never teach the actual word "come." Yet these dogs will race to respond to a person who uses the dog's name followed by "Where are you?" For example, a woman has a 12-year-old companion dog who went blind, but who never fails to locate her owner when asked, "Where are you?"

Children particularly love to play this game with their dogs. Children can hide in smaller places like a shower or bathtub, behind a bed or under a table. The dog needs to work a little bit harder to find these hiding places, but, when he does, he loves to celebrate with a treat and a tussle with a favorite youngster.

A Havanese heeling at his handler's side is completely in tune to the direction and tempo of the handler.

TEACHING HEEL

Heeling means that the dog walks beside the owner without pulling. It takes time and patience on the owner's part to succeed at teaching the dog that he (the owner) will not proceed unless the dog is walking calmly beside him. Pulling out ahead on the lead is definitely not acceptable.

HEELING WELL

Teach your dog to heel in an enclosed area. Once you think the dog will obey reliably and you want to attempt advanced obedience exercises such as off-lead heeling, test him in a fenced-in area so he cannot run away.

Begin with holding the lead in your left hand as the dog sits beside your left leg. Move the loop end of the lead to your right hand but keep your left hand short on the lead so it keeps the dog in close next to you. Say "Heel" and step forward on your left foot. Keep the dog close to you and take three steps. Stop and have the dog sit next to you in what we now call the heel position. Praise verbally, but do not touch the dog. Hesitate a moment and begin again with "Heel," taking three steps and stopping, at which point the dog is told to sit again.

Your goal here is to have the dog walk those three steps without pulling on the lead. When he will walk calmly beside you for three steps without pulling, increase the number of steps you take to five. When he will walk politely beside you while you take five steps, you can increase the length of your walk to ten steps. Keep increasing the length of your stroll until the dog will walk quietly beside you without pulling as long as you want him to heel. When you stop heeling, indicate to the dog that the exercise is over by verbally praising as you pet him and say "OK, good dog." The "OK" is used as a release word, meaning that the exercise is finished and the dog is free to relax.

If you are dealing with a dog who insists on pulling you around, simply "put on your brakes" and stand your ground until the dog realizes that the two of you are not going anywhere until he is beside you and moving at your pace, not his. It may take some time just standing there to convince the dog that you are the leader and you will be the one to decide on the direction and speed of your travel.

Each time the dog looks up at you or slows down to give a slack lead between the two of you, quietly praise him and say, "Good heel. Good dog." Eventually, the dog will begin to respond and within a few days he will be walking politely beside you without pulling on the lead. At first, the training sessions should be kept short and very positive; soon the dog will be able to walk nicely with you for increasingly longer distances. Remember also to give the dog free time and the opportunity to run and play when you are done with heel practice.

WEANING OFF FOOD IN TRAINING

Food is used in training new behaviors. Once the dog under-stands what behavior goes with a specific command, it is time to start weaning him off the food treats. At first, give a treat after each exercise. Then, start to give a treat only after every other exercise. Mix up the times when you offer a food reward and the

OBEDIENCE SCHOOL

A basic obedience beginner's class usually lasts for six to eight weeks. Dog and owner attend an hour-long lesson once a week and practice for a few minutes, several times a day, each day at home. If done properly, the whole procedure will result in a well-mannered dog and an owner who delights in living with a pet that is eager to please and enjoys doing things with his owner.

times when you only offer praise so that the dog will never know when he is going to receive both food and praise and when he is going to receive only praise. This is called a variable-ratio reward system and it proves successful because there is always the chance that the owner will produce a treat, so the dog never stops trying for that reward. No matter what, *always* give verbal praise.

OBEDIENCE CLASSES

It is a good idea to enroll in an obedience class if one is available in your area. If yours is a show dog, handling classes would be more appropriate. Many areas have dog clubs that offer basic obedience training as well as preparatory classes for obedience competition. There are also local dog trainers who offer similar classes.

At obedience trials, dogs can earn titles at various levels of competition. The beginning levels of competition include basic behaviors such as sit, down, heel, etc. The more advanced levels of competition include jumping, retrieving, scent discrimination and signal work. The advanced levels require a dog and owner to put a lot of time and effort into their training, and the titles that can be earned at these levels of competition are very prestigious.

Gaiting in the show ring is time for the Havanese to display his lively, confident character.

OTHER ACTIVITIES FOR LIFE

Whether a dog is trained in the structured environment of a class or alone with his owner at home, there are many activities that can bring fun and rewards to both owner and dog once they have mastered basic control.

Teaching the dog to help out around the home, in the yard or on the farm provides great satisfaction to both dog and owner. In addition, the dog's help makes life a little easier for his owner

A BORN PRODIGY

Occasionally, a dog and owner who have not attended formal classes have been able to earn entry-level titles by obtaining competition rules and regulations from a local kennel club and practicing on their own to a degree of perfection. Obtaining the higher level titles, however, almost always requires extensive training under the tutelage of experienced instructors. In addition, the more difficult levels require more specialized equipment whereas the lower levels do not.

Havanese trained for the show ring must respond effortlessly to their handlers' leads. For show dogs, heeling is an obvious requirement if the dogs are to display proper gait.

and raises his stature as a valued companion to his family. It helps give the dog a purpose by occupying his mind and providing an outlet for his energy.

If you are interested in participating in organized competition with your Havanese, there are activities other than obedience in which you and your dog can become involved. Agility is a popular and fun sport where dogs run through an obstacle course that includes various jumps, tunnels and other exercises to test the dog's speed and coordination. The owners run through the course beside their dogs to give commands and to guide them through the course. Although competitive, the focus is on fun—it's fun to do, fun to watch, and great exercise for owner and dog.

HAVANESE

Dogs suffer from many of the same physical illnesses as people and might even share many of the same psychological problems. Since people usually know more about human diseases than canine maladies, many of the terms used in this chapter will be familiar but not necessarily those used by veterinarians. For example, we will use the familiar term *x-ray* instead of *radiograph*. We will also use the familiar term *symptoms*, even though dogs don't have symptoms, which are verbal descriptions of something the patient feels or observes himself

that he regards as abnormal. Dogs have *clinical signs* since they cannot speak, so we have to look for these clinical signs...but we still use the term *symptoms* in the book.

Medicine is a constantly changing art, with of course scientific input as well. Things alter as we learn more and more about basic sciences such as genetics and biochemistry, and have use of

more sophisticated imaging techniques like Computer Aided Tomography (CAT scans) or Magnetic Resonance Imaging (MRI scans). There is academic dispute about many canine maladies, so different veterinarians treat them in different ways; for example, some vets place a greater emphasis on surgical treatment options than others.

SELECTING A QUALIFIED VET

Your selection of a veterinarian should be based not only upon personality and ability with small dogs but also upon convenience to your home. You want a vet who is close because you might have emergencies or need to make multiple visits for treatments. You want a vet who has services that you might require such as a boarding kennel and grooming facilities, as well as the latest pet supplies and a good reputation for ability and responsiveness. There is nothing more frustrating than having to wait a day or more to get a response

Before you buy your Havanese, interview the vets in your area and select the one who best suits your needs. Discuss his schedule of fees, policies and office and emergency hours.

Breakdown of Veterinary Income by Category

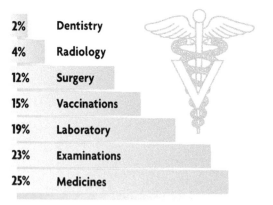

2%	Dentistry
4%	Radiology
12%	Surgery
15%	Vaccinations
19%	Laboratory
23%	Examinations
25%	Medicines

A typical vet's income, categorized according to services performed. This survey dealt with small-animal (pets) practices.

from your veterinarian.

All veterinarians are licensed and their diplomas and/or certificates should be displayed in their waiting rooms. Most vets deal with basic health issues like infections, injuries, vaccinations, routine surgery, etc. There are, however, many veterinary specialties that require further studies and internships. For example, there are specialists in heart problems (veterinary cardiologists), skin problems (veterinary dermatologists), teeth and gum problems (veterinary dentists), eye problems (veterinary ophthalmologists), and x-rays (veterinary radiologists), and surgeons who have specialties in bones, muscles or certain organs. When the problem affecting your dog is serious, your vet will refer you to a specialist in the appropriate field. It is not unusual or impudent to get another

medical opinion, although it is always courteous to advise the vets concerned about this. You might also want to compare costs among several vets. Sophisticated health care and veterinary services can be very costly. Don't be bashful about discussing these costs with your vet or his staff. It is not infrequent that important decisions are based upon financial considerations.

PREVENTATIVE MEDICINE
It is much easier, less costly and more effective to practice preventative medicine than to fight bouts of illness and disease. Properly bred puppies come from parents that were selected based upon their genetic-disease profiles. Their dam should have been vaccinated, free of all internal and external parasites and properly nourished. For these reasons, a visit to the vet who cared for the dam is recommended. The dam can pass on disease resistance to her puppies, which can last for eight to ten weeks. She can also pass on parasites and many infections. That's why you should learn about the dam's health.

WEANING TO FIVE MONTHS OLD
Puppies should be weaned by the time they are about two months old. A puppy that remains for *at least* eight weeks with his mother and littermates usually adapts better to other dogs and people

First Aid at a Glance

Burns
Place the affected area under cool water; use ice if only a small area is burnt.

Bee stings/Insect bites
Apply ice to relieve swelling; antihistamine dosed properly.

Animal bites
Clean any bleeding area; apply pressure until bleeding subsides; go to the vet.

Spider bites
Use cold compress and a pressurized pack to inhibit venom's spreading.

Antifreeze poisoning
Induce vomiting with hydrogen peroxide. Seek *immediate* veterinary help!

Fish hooks
Removal best handled by vet; hook must be cut in order to remove.

Snake bites
Pack ice around bite; contact vet quickly; identify snake for proper antivenin.

Car accident
Move dog from roadway with blanket; seek veterinary aid.

Shock
Calm the dog; keep him warm; seek immediate veterinary help.

Nosebleed
Apply cold compress to the nose; apply pressure to any visible abrasion.

Bleeding
Apply pressure above the area; treat wound by applying a cotton pack.

Heat stroke
Submerge dog in cold bath; cool down with fresh air and water; go to the vet.

Frostbite/Hypothermia
Warm the dog with a warm bath, electric blankets or hot water bottles.

Abrasions
Clean the wound and wash out thoroughly with fresh water; apply antiseptic.

 Remember: an injured dog may attempt to bite a helping hand from fear and confusion. Always muzzle the dog before trying to offer assistance.

later in his life.

Sometimes new owners have their puppy examined by a vet immediately, which is a good idea. The puppy will have his teeth examined and his skeletal conformation and general health checked prior to certification by the vet. Puppies in certain breeds have problems with their kneecaps, cataracts and other eye problems, heart murmurs and undescended testicles. Your vet might also have training in temperament evaluation. Your pup's vaccination schedule will be set up at the first visit.

VACCINATION SCHEDULING
Most vaccinations are given by injection and should only be done by a vet. Both he and you should

KEEPING MOM HEALTHY
Caring for the puppy starts before the puppy is born by keeping the dam healthy and well-nourished. Most puppies have worms, even if they are not evident, so a worming program is essential. The worms continually shed eggs except during their dormant stage, when they just rest in the tissues of the puppy. During this stage they are not evident during a routine examination.

keep a record of the date of the injection, the identification of the vaccine and the amount given. Some vets give a first vaccination at six weeks, but most dog breeders prefer the course not to commence until about eight weeks because of negating any antibodies passed on by the dam. The vaccination scheduling is usually based on a two- to four-week cycle. You must take your vet's advice as to when to vaccinate as this may differ according to the vaccine used.

Most vaccinations immunize your puppy against viruses. The usual vaccines contain immunizing doses of several different viruses such as distemper, parvovirus, parainfluenza and hepatitis. There are other vaccines available when the puppy is at risk. You should rely upon professional advice. This is especially true for the booster-shot program.

Most vaccination programs require a booster when the puppy is a year old and once a year thereafter. In some cases, circumstances may require more or less frequent immunizations.

The most serious diseases that affect the Havanese also affect any other dog: parvovirus, adenovirus, coronavirus, distemper, hepatitis, leptospirosis and rabies. All these diseases are fatal in more than 90% of cases. The only sure way to prevent them is to vaccinate your dog. Always ask the breeder for

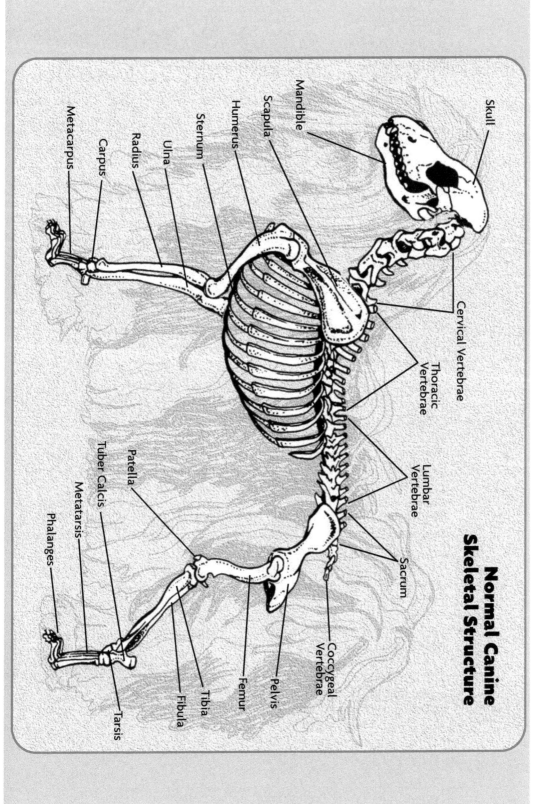

**Normal Canine
Skeletal Structure**

Skull

Cervical Vertebrae

Mandible

Scapula

Humerus

Sternum

Radius

Ulna

Carpus

Metacarpus

Thoracic
Vertebrae

Lumbar
Vertebrae

Sacrum

Coccygeal
Vertebrae

Pelvis

Femur

Tibia

Fibula

Patella

Tuber Calcis

Metatarsis

Phalanges

Tarsis

HEALTH AND VACCINATION SCHEDULE

Age in Weeks:	6th	8th	10th	12th	14th	16th	20-24th	52nd
Worm Control	✔	✔	✔	✔	✔	✔	✔	
Neutering							✔	
Heartworm		✔		✔		✔	✔	
Parvovirus	✔		✔		✔		✔	✔
Distemper		✔		✔		✔		✔
Hepatitis		✔		✔		✔		✔
Leptospirosis								✔
Parainfluenza	✔		✔		✔			✔
Dental Examination		✔					✔	✔
Complete Physical		✔					✔	✔
Coronavirus				✔			✔	✔
Canine Cough	✔							
Hip Dysplasia								✔
Rabies							✔	

Vaccinations are not instantly effective. It takes about two weeks for the dog's immune system to develop antibodies. Most vaccinations require annual booster shots. Your vet should guide you in this regard.

worming and vaccination certificates in addition to the pedigree.

Canine cough, more formally known as tracheobronchitis, is treated with a vaccine that is sprayed into the dog's nostrils. Canine cough is usually included in routine vaccination, but this is often not so effective as for other major diseases.

FIVE MONTHS TO ONE YEAR OF AGE
Unless you intend to breed or show your dog, neutering the puppy around six months of age is recommended. Discuss this with your vet; most professionals advise neutering the puppy. Neutering/spaying has proven to be extremely beneficial to both dogs and bitches. Besides eliminating the possibility of pregnancy and pyometra in bitches and testicular cancer in males, it greatly reduces the risk of (but

VACCINE ALLERGIES
Vaccines do not work all the time. Sometimes dogs are allergic to them and many times the antibodies, which are supposed to be stimulated by the vaccine, just are not produced. You should keep your dog in the veterinary clinic for an hour after he is vaccinated to be sure there are no allergic reactions.

does not prevent) breast cancer in bitches and prostate cancer in male dogs.

Your vet should provide your puppy with a thorough dental evaluation at six months of age, ascertaining whether all of the permanent teeth have erupted properly. A home dental-care regimen should be initiated at six months, including brushing weekly and providing good dental devices (such as nylon bones). Regular dental care promotes healthy teeth, fresh breath and a longer life.

DOGS OLDER THAN ONE YEAR
Continue to visit the vet at least once a year. There is no such disease as old age, but bodily functions do change with age. The eyes and ears are no longer as efficient. Liver, kidney and intestinal functions often decline. Proper dietary changes, recommended by your vet, can make life more pleasant for the aging Havanese and you.

Other less serious health problems in adult dogs include eye and ear infections that can occur if you neglect cleaning your dog's

DISEASE REFERENCE CHART

	What is it?	What causes it?	Symptoms
Leptospirosis	Severe disease that affects the internal organs; can be spread to people.	A bacterium, which is often carried by rodents, that enters through mucous membranes and spreads quickly throughout the body.	Range from fever, vomiting and loss of appetite in less severe cases to shock, irreversible kidney damage and possibly death in most severe cases.
Rabies	Potentially deadly virus that infects warm-blooded mammals.	Bite from a carrier of the virus, mainly wild animals.	1st stage: dog exhibits change in behavior, fear. 2nd stage: dog's behavior becomes more aggressive. 3rd stage: loss of coordination, trouble with bodily functions.
Parvovirus	Highly contagious virus, potentially deadly.	Ingestion of the virus, which is usually spread through the feces of infected dogs.	Most common: severe diarrhea. Also vomiting, fatigue, lack of appetite.
Canine cough	Contagious respiratory infection.	Combination of types of bacteria and virus. Most common: *Bordetella bronchiseptica* bacteria and parainfluenza virus.	Chronic cough.
Distemper	Disease primarily affecting respiratory and nervous system.	Virus that is related to the human measles virus.	Mild symptoms such as fever, lack of appetite and mucus secretion progress to evidence of brain damage, "hard pad."
Hepatitis	Virus primarily affecting the liver.	Canine adenovirus type I (CAV-1). Enters system when dog breathes in particles.	Lesser symptoms include listlessness, diarrhea, vomiting. More severe symptoms include "blue-eye" (clumps of virus in eye).
Coronavirus	Virus resulting in digestive problems.	Virus is spread through infected dog's feces.	Stomach upset evidenced by lack of appetite, vomiting, diarrhea.

eyes and are careless about water entering the ears during bathing. A good way of detecting ear problems is to smell his ears, since any strange odor may indicate that something's wrong. Another method is to place your own ear next to your dog's while you rub the outside of his ear where it joins the head. If the ear has accumulated water or any other liquid, you will easily hear it moving inside the ear.

Skin irritations are another problem and some Havanese are accustomed to biting their skin in certain areas. The saliva that accumulates moistens that part of the skin and causes the hair to stick to it, which may cause a small epidermal eruption that can easily be treated by shaving the irritated area and

PUPPY VACCINATIONS
Your veterinarian will probably recommend that your puppy be fully vaccinated before you take him outside. There are airborne diseases, parasite eggs in the grass and unexpected visits from other dogs that might be dangerous to your puppy's health. Other dogs are the most harmful reservoir of pathogenic organisms, as everything they have can be transmitted to your puppy.

applying the indicated medicine.

The routine of going over your pet at least once a week is very useful, for it permits you to detect any problem before it becomes serious. Remember that he can't talk, that he will tolerate considerable pain and that, as an animal, he tends to be more stoic about his problems than we humans are.

Check his mouth to make sure there are no residues that could cause future gum problems. Check between the toes and pads of the feet to find any hard little objects that may become lodged there.

Dogs occasionally have diarrhea when their diet is changed, when they overeat or when they drink too much milk, especially if they aren't accustomed to it. This is normal. But never overlook diarrhea. Many diseases can begin with an apparently insignificant case of diarrhea. However, if your dog is properly vaccinated, there's a large measure of security that he won't suffer from any of them.

SKIN PROBLEMS IN HAVANESE
Veterinarians are consulted by dog owners for skin problems more than for any other group of diseases or maladies. Dogs' skin is almost as sensitive as human skin and both can suffer from almost the same ailments (though the

occurrence of acne in most dogs is rare). For this reason, veterinary dermatology has developed into a specialty practiced by many vets.

Since many skin problems have visual symptoms that are almost identical, it requires the skill of an experienced veterinary dermatologist to identify and cure many of the more severe skin disorders. Pet shops sell many treatments for skin problems but most of the treatments are directed at symptoms and not the underlying problem(s). If your dog is suffering from a skin disorder, you should seek professional assistance as quickly as possible. As with all diseases, the earlier a problem is identified and treated, the more likely is a complete cure.

Auto-Immune Skin Conditions

Auto-immune skin conditions are commonly referred to as being allergic to yourself, while allergies are usually inflammatory reactions to an outside stimulus. Auto-immune diseases cause serious damage to the tissues that are involved.

The best known auto-immune disease is lupus, which affects people as well as dogs. The symptoms are variable and may affect the kidneys, bones, blood chemistry and skin. It can be fatal to both dogs and humans, though it is not thought to be transmissible.

DENTAL HEALTH

A dental examination is in order when the dog is between six months and one year of age so that any permanent teeth that have erupted incorrectly can be corrected. It is important to begin a brushing routine at home, using dental-care products like special toothpaste and toothbrushes made for dogs. Durable nylon and safe edible chews should be a part of your puppy's arsenal for good health, good teeth and pleasant breath. The vast majority of dogs three to four years old and older has diseases of the gums from lack of dental attention. Using the various types of dental chews can be very effective in controlling dental plaque.

It is usually successfully treated with cortisone, prednisone or similar corticosteroid, but extensive use of these drugs can have harmful side effects.

Hereditary Skin Disorders

Veterinary dermatologists are currently researching a number of skin disorders that are believed to have a hereditary basis. These inherited diseases are transmitted by both parents, who appear (phenotypically) normal but have a recessive gene for the disease, meaning that they carry, but are not affected by, the disease. These diseases pose serious problems to breeders because in some instances there are no methods of identifying carriers. Often the secondary diseases associated with these skin conditions are even more debilitating than the skin disorders themselves, including cancers and respiratory problems.

Among the hereditary skin disorders, for which the mode of inheritance is known, are acrodermatitis, cutaneous asthenia (Ehlers-Danlos syndrome), sebaceous adenitis, cyclic hematopoiesis, dermatomyositis, IgA deficiency, color dilution alopecia and nodular dermatofibrosis. Some of these disorders are limited to one or two breeds, while others affect a large number of breeds. All inherited diseases must be diagnosed and treated by a veterinary specialist.

PARASITE BITES

Many of us are allergic to insect bites. The bites itch, erupt and may even become infected. Dogs have the same reaction to fleas, ticks and/or mites. When an insect lands on you, you have the chance to whisk it away with your hand.

FAT OR FICTION?

The myth that dogs need extra fat in their diets can be harmful. Should your vet recommend extra fat, use safflower oil instead of animal oils. Safflower oil has been shown to be less likely to cause allergic reactions.

Unfortunately, when your dog is bitten by a flea, tick or mite, he can only scratch it away or bite it. By the time the dog has been bitten, the parasite has done some of its damage. It may also have laid eggs to cause further problems in the near future. The itching from parasite bites is probably due to the saliva injected into the site when the parasite sucks the dog's blood.

AIRBORNE ALLERGIES

Just as humans have hay fever, rose fever and other fevers from which they suffer during the pollinating season, many dogs suffer from the same allergies. When the pollen count is high, your dog might suffer but don't expect him to sneeze and have a runny nose like a human would. Dogs react to pollen allergies the same way they react to fleas—they scratch and bite themselves.

Dogs, like humans, can be tested for allergens. Discuss the testing with your veterinary dermatologist.

FOOD PROBLEMS

Dogs are allergic to many foods that are best-sellers and highly recommended by breeders and vets. Changing the brand of food that you buy may not eliminate the problem if the element to which the dog is allergic is contained in the new brand.

Recognizing a food allergy is difficult. Humans vomit or have rashes when they eat a food to which they are allergic. Dogs neither vomit nor (usually) develop a rash. They react in the same manner as they do to an airborne or flea allergy: they itch, scratch and bite, thus making the diagnosis extremely difficult. While pollen allergies and parasite bites are seasonal, food allergies are year-round problems.

FOOD INTOLERANCE

Food intolerance is the inability of the dog to completely digest certain foods. For example, puppies that may have done very well on their mother's milk may not do well on cow's milk. The result of this food intolerance may be loose bowels, passing gas and stomach pains. These are the only obvious symptoms of food intolerance and that makes diagnosis difficult.

TREATING FOOD PROBLEMS

It is possible to handle food allergies and ood intolerance yourself. Put your dog on a diet that he has never had. Obviously, if he has never eaten this new food, he can't have been allergic or intolerant of it.

Start with a single ingredient that is not in the dog's diet at the present time. Ingredients like chopped beef or chicken are common in dog's diets, so try something more exotic like rabbit, pheasant or another source of quality potein. Keep the dog on this diet (with no additives) for a month. If the symptoms of food allergy or intolerance disappear, chances are your dog has a food allergy.

Don't think that the single ingredient cured the problem. You still must find a suitable diet and ascertain which ingredient in the old diet was objectionable. This is most easily done by adding ingredients to the new diet one at a time. Let the dog stay on the modified diet for a month before you add another ingredient. Eventually, you will determine the ingredient that caused the adverse reaction.

An alternative method is to carefully study the ingredients in the diet to which your dog is allergic or intolerable. Identify the main ingredient in this diet and eliminate the main ingredient by buying a different food that does not have that ingredient. Keep experimenting until the symptoms disappear after one month on the new diet.

GENETIC DISEASES OF THE HAVANESE

Thanks to the advances of science and technology, it is now possible to identify a series of diseases of genetic origin in dogs. This imposes an important responsibility on breeders, who have to be aware of and make every effort to eradicate the diseases that can affect the animals they breed. Almost every breed is subject to one or more.

Ask the breeder or owner from whom you acquire your dog to give you some certification that the pup's parents and grandparents are healthy specimens; otherwise, you run the risk of having an animal that will give you only headaches instead of joy.

It's also advisable to take your newly acquired pup to a veterinarian for a complete examination. If any defects show up, you can then decide whether to return the dog or keep it. An animal with genetic defects or diseases should never be used for breeding.

Among the diseases of genetic origin in the Havanese are cataracts and PRA (progressive retina atrophy), which usually causes blindness in the afflicted animal. They have been detected in Havanese bred in the United States and in some European countries.

The only way to detect PRA is through a special test, although the dog often presents symptoms such as increased size of the pupil, limited vision and even blindness. This disease is very hard to eradicate, since it often occurs in adulthood, when the diagnosis is too late to prevent reproduction. Nevertheless, because of its recurrence in the US, it is of vital importance to examine the

> **THE PROTEIN QUESTION**
> Your dog's protein needs are changeable. High activity level, stress, climate and other physical factors may require your dog to have more protein in his diet. Check with your veterinarian.

entire litter early on, and then check each dog annually to make sure the problem doesn't exist.

Complicating the eradication of PRA is the fact that the gene responsible for producing it is a recessive gene, so the dog can be a carrier without actually having the disease. If a carrier is bred with a healthy animal, the offspring will be healthy, but 50% will be carriers. When two apparently healthy carriers are bred, the situation is further complicated as 50% of the litter will be carriers and 25% will be diseased. In an even worse case, that of breeding a healthy dog with a diseased dog, the result will be that 100% of the litter will be carriers although they appear to be healthy.

These numbers may sound a bit schematic, but they give us an idea of how important it is to pay attention to this problem. Once the recessive gene for PRA has entered the breeding line, it will be passed from generation to generation until another recessive gene for PRA is encountered. Only then will the disease appear as proof that the line was actually affected.

Number-One Killer Disease in Dogs: CANCER

In every age, there is a word associated with a disease or plague that causes humans to shudder. In the 21st century, that word is "cancer." Just as cancer is the leading cause of death in humans, it claims nearly half the lives of dogs that die from a natural disease as well as half the dogs that die over the age of ten years.

Described as a genetic disease, cancer becomes a greater risk as the dog ages. Vets and dog owners have become increasingly aware of the threat of cancer to dogs. Statistics reveal that one dog in every five will develop cancer, the most common of which is skin cancer. Many cancers, including prostate, ovarian and breast cancer, can be avoided by spaying and neutering our dogs around the age of six months.

Early detection of cancer can save or extend a dog's life, so it is absolutely vital for owners to have their dogs examined by a qualified vet or oncologist immediately upon detection of any abnormality. Certain dietary guidelines have also proven to reduce the onset and spread of cancer. Foods based on fish rather than beef, due to the presence of Omega-3 fatty acids, are recommended. Other amino acids such as glutamine have significant benefits for canines, particularly those breeds that show a greater susceptibility to cancer.

Cancer management and treatments promise hope for future generations of canines. Since the disease is genetic, breeders should never breed a dog whose parents, grandparents and any related siblings have developed cancer. It is difficult to know whether to exclude an otherwise healthy dog from a breeding program as the disease does not manifest itself until the dog's senior years.

RECOGNIZE CANCER WARNING SIGNS

Since early detection can possibly rescue your dog from becoming a cancer statistic, it is essential for owners to recognize the possible signs and seek the assistance of a qualified professional.

- Abnormal bumps or lumps that continue to grow
- Bleeding or discharge from any body cavity
- Persistent stiffness or lameness
- Recurrent sores or sores that do not heal
- Inappetence
- Breathing difficulties
- Weight loss
- Bad breath or odors
- General malaise and fatigue
- Eating and swallowing problems
- Difficulty urinating and defecating

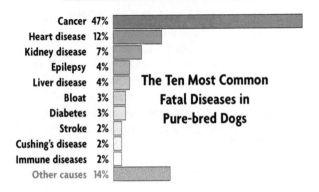

Disease	%
Cancer	47%
Heart disease	12%
Kidney disease	7%
Epilepsy	4%
Liver disease	4%
Bloat	3%
Diabetes	3%
Stroke	2%
Cushing's disease	2%
Immune diseases	2%
Other causes	14%

The Ten Most Common Fatal Diseases in Pure-bred Dogs

A male dog flea, *Ctenocephalides canis.*

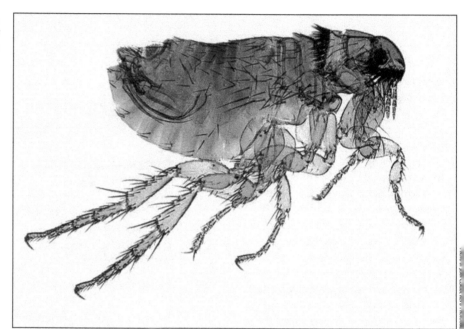

EXTERNAL PARASITES

FLEAS

Of all the problems to which dogs are prone, none is more well known and frustrating than fleas. Flea infestation is relatively simple to cure but difficult to prevent. Parasites that are harbored inside the body are a bit more difficult to eradicate but they are easier to control.

To control flea infestation, you have to understand the flea's life cycle. Fleas are often thought of as a summertime problem, but centrally heated homes have changed the patterns and fleas can be found at any time of the year. The most effective method of flea control is a two-stage approach: one stage to kill the adult fleas, and the other to control the development of pre-adult fleas. Unfortunately, no single active ingredient is effective against all stages of the life cycle.

FLEA KILLER CAUTION— "POISON"

Flea-killers are poisonous. You should not spray these toxic chemicals on areas of a dog's body that he licks, including his genitals and his face. Flea killers taken internally are a better answer, but check with your vet in case internal therapy is not advised for your dog.

LIFE CYCLE STAGES

During its life, a flea will pass through four life stages: egg, larva, pupa or nymph and adult. The adult stage is the most visible and irritating stage of the flea life cycle, and this is why the majority of flea-control products concentrate on this stage. The fact is that adult fleas account for only 1% of the total flea population, and the other 99% exist in pre-adult stages, i.e., eggs, larvae and nymphs. The pre-adult stages are barely visible to the naked eye.

THE LIFE CYCLE OF THE FLEA

Eggs are laid on the dog, usually in quantities of about 20 or 30, several times a day. The adult female flea must have a blood meal before each egg-laying session. When first laid, the eggs will cling to the dog's hair, as the eggs are still moist. However, they will quickly dry out and fall from the dog, especially if the dog moves around or scratches. Many eggs will fall off in the dog's favorite area or an area in which he spends a lot of time, such as his bed.

Once the eggs fall from the dog onto the carpet or furniture, they will hatch into larvae. This takes from one to ten days. Larvae are not particularly mobile and will usually travel only a few inches from where they hatch. However, they do have a tendency to move away from bright light and heavy

EN GARDE:
CATCHING FLEAS OFF GUARD!
Consider the following ways to arm yourself against fleas:
- Add a small amount of pennyroyal or eucalyptus oil to your dog's bath. These natural remedies repel fleas.
- Supplement your dog's food with fresh garlic (minced or grated) and a hearty amount of brewer's yeast, both of which ward off fleas.
- Use a flea comb on your dog daily. Submerge fleas in a cup of bleach to kill them quickly.
- Confine the dog to only a few rooms to limit the spread of fleas in the home.
- Vacuum daily...and get all of the crevices! Dispose of the bag every few days until the problem is under control.
- Wash your dog's bedding daily. Cover cushions where your dog sleeps with towels, and wash the towels often.

traffic—under furniture and behind doors are common places to find high quantities of flea larvae.

The flea larvae feed on dead organic matter, including adult flea feces, until they are ready to change into adult fleas. Fleas will usually remain as larvae for around seven days. After this period, the larvae will pupate into protective pupae. While inside the pupae, the larvae will undergo

Fleas have been measured as being able to jump 300,000 times and can jump over 150 times their length in any direction, including straight up.

metamorphosis and change into adult fleas. This can take as little time as a few days, but the adult fleas can remain inside the pupae waiting to hatch for up to two years. The pupae are signaled to hatch by certain stimuli, such as physical pressure—the pupae's being stepped on, heat from an animal's lying on the pupae or increased carbon-dioxide levels and vibrations—indicating that a suitable host is available.

Once hatched, the adult flea must feed within a few days. Once the adult flea finds a host, it will not leave voluntarily. It only becomes dislodged by grooming or the host animal's scratching.

The adult flea will remain on the host for the duration of its life unless forcibly removed.

TREATING THE ENVIRONMENT AND THE DOG

Treating fleas should be a two-pronged attack. First, the environment needs to be treated; this includes carpets and furniture, especially the dog's bedding and areas underneath furniture. The environment should be treated with a household spray containing an Insect Growth Regulator (IGR) and an insecticide to kill the adult fleas. Most IGRs are effective against eggs and larvae; they actually mimic the fleas' own hormones and stop the eggs and larvae from developing into adult fleas. There are currently no treatments available to attack the pupa stage of the life cycle, so the adult insecticide is used to kill the newly hatched adult fleas before they find a host. Most IGRs are active for many months, while

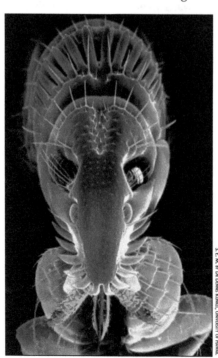

A scanning electron micrograph of a dog or cat flea, *Ctenocephalides*, magnified more than 100x. This image has been colorized for effect.

THE LIFE CYCLE OF THE FLEA

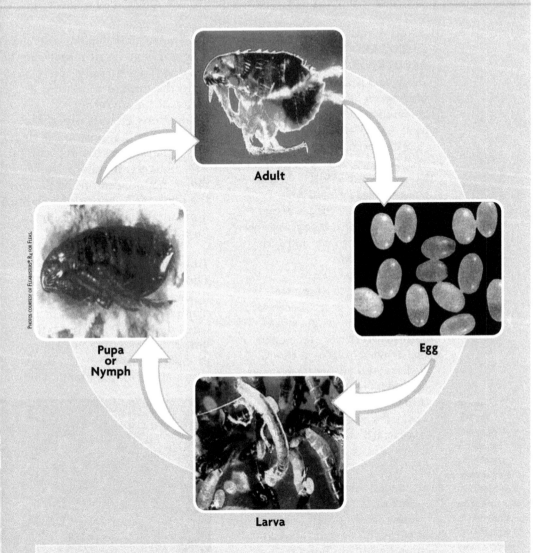

Adult

Egg

Larva

Pupa
or
Nymph

PHOTOS COURTESY OF FLEABUSTERS® Rx FOR FLEAS.

Fleas have been around for millions of years and have adapted to changing host animals. They are able to go through a complete life cycle in less than one month or they can extend their lives to almost two years by remaining as pupae or cocoons. They do not need blood or any other food for up to 20 months.

INSECT GROWTH REGULATOR (IGR)

Two types of products should be used when treating fleas—a product to treat the pet and a product to treat the home. Adult fleas represent less than 1% of the flea population. The pre-adult fleas (eggs, larvae and pupae) represent more than 99% of the flea population and are found in the environment; it is in the case of pre-adult fleas that products containing an Insect Growth Regulator (IGR) should be used in the home.

IGRs are a new class of compounds used to prevent the development of insects. They do not kill the insect outright, but instead use the insect's biology against it to stop it from completing its growth. Products that contain methoprene are the world's first and leading IGRs. Used to control fleas and other insects, this type of IGR will stop flea larvae from developing and protect the house for up to seven months.

The American dog tick, *Dermacentor variabilis*, is probably the most common tick found on dogs. Look at the strength in its eight legs! No wonder it's hard to detach them.

adult insecticides are only active for a few days.

When treating with a household spray, it is a good idea to vacuum before applying the product. This stimulates as many pupae as possible to hatch into adult fleas. The vacuum cleaner should also be treated with an insecticide to prevent the eggs and larvae that have been collected in the vacuum bag from hatching.

The second stage of treatment is to apply an adult insecticide to the dog. Traditionally, this would be in the form of a collar or a spray, but more recent innovations include digestible insecticides that poison the fleas when they ingest the dog's blood. Alternatively, there are drops that, when placed on the back of the dog's neck, spread throughout the hair and skin to kill adult fleas.

TICKS

Though not as common as fleas, ticks are found all over the tropical and temperate world. They don't bite, like fleas; they harpoon. They dig their sharp proboscis (nose) into the dog's skin and drink the blood. Their

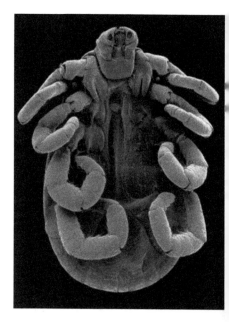

only food and drink is dog's blood. Dogs can get Lyme disease, Rocky Mountain spotted fever, tick bite paralysis and many other diseases from ticks. They may live where fleas are found and they like to hide in cracks or seams in walls. They are controlled the same way fleas are controlled.

The American dog tick, *Dermacentor variabilis*, may well be the most common dog tick in many geographical areas, especially those areas where the climate is hot and humid. Most dog ticks have life expectancies of a week to six months, depending upon climatic conditions. They can neither jump nor fly, but they can crawl slowly and can range up to 16 feet to reach a sleeping or unsuspecting dog.

MITES

Just as fleas and ticks can be problematic for your dog, mites can also lead to an itchy nuisance. Microscopic in size, mites are related to ticks and generally take up permanent residence on their host animal—in this case, your dog! The term *mange* refers to any infestation caused by one of the mighty mites, of which there are six varieties that concern dog owners.

Demodex mites cause a condition known as demodicosis

DEER-TICK CROSSING
The great outdoors may be fun for your dog, but it also is a home to dangerous ticks. Deer ticks carry a bacterium known as *Borrelia burgdorferi* and are most active in the autumn and spring. When infections are caught early, penicillin and tetracycline are effective antibiotics, but, if left untreated, the bacteria may cause neurological, kidney and cardiac problems as well as long-term trouble with walking and painful joints.

The head of an American dog tick, *Dermacentor variabilis*, enlarged and colorized for effect.

(sometimes called red mange or follicular mange), in which the mites live in the dog's hair follicles and sebaceous glands in larger-than-normal numbers. This type of mange is commonly passed from the dam to her puppies and usually shows up on the puppies' muzzles, though demodicosis is not transferable from one normal dog to another. Most dogs recover from this type of mange without any treatment, though topical therapies are commonly prescribed by the vet.

The *Cheyletiellosis* mite is the

hook-mouthed culprit associated with "walking dandruff," a condition that affects dogs as well as cats and rabbits. This mite lives on the surface of the animal's skin and is readily transferable through direct or indirect contact with an affected animal. The dandruff is present in the form of scaly skin, which may or may not be itchy. If not treated, this mange can affect a whole kennel of dogs and can be spread to humans as well.

The *Sarcoptes* mite causes intense itching on the dog in the form of a condition known as scabies or sarcoptic mange. The cycle of the *Sarcoptes* mite lasts about three weeks, and the mites live in the top layer of the dog's skin (epidermis), preferably in areas with little hair. Scabies is highly contagious and can be passed to humans. Sometimes an allergic reaction to the mite worsens the severe itching associated with sarcoptic mange.

Ear mites, *Otodectes cynotis*, lead to otodectic mange, which most commonly affects the outer ear canal of the dog, though other areas can be affected as well. Dogs with ear-mite infestation commonly scratch at their ears, causing further irritation, and shake their heads. Dark brown droppings in the outer ear confirm the diagnosis. Your vet can prescribe a treatment to flush out the ears and kill any eggs in the ears. A complete month of treatment is necessary to cure the mange.

Two other mites, less common in dogs, include *Dermanyssus gallinae* (the poultry or red mite) and *Eutrombicula alfreddugesi* (the North American mite associated with trombiculidiasis or chigger infestation). The poultry mite frequently lives on chickens, but can transfer to dogs who spend time near farm animals. Chigger

NOT A DROP TO DRINK

Never allow your dog to swim in polluted water or public areas where water quality can be suspect. Even perfectly clear water can harbor parasites, many of which can cause serious to fatal illnesses in canines. Areas inhabited by water-fowl and other wildlife are especially dangerous.

infestation affects dogs in the Central US who have exposure to woodlands. The types of mange caused by both of these mites are treatable by vets.

INTERNAL PARASITES

Most animals—fishes, birds and mammals, including dogs and humans—have worms and other parasites that live inside their bodies. According to Dr. Herbert R. Axelrod, the fish pathologist, there are two kinds of parasites: dumb and smart. The smart parasites live in peaceful cooperation with their hosts (symbiosis), while the dumb parasites kill their hosts. Most worm infections are relatively easy to control. If they are not controlled, they weaken the host dog to the point that other medical problems occur, but they do not kill the host as dumb parasites would.

The brown dog tick, *Rhipicephalus sanguineus*, is an uncommon but annoying tick found on dogs.

PHOTO BY CAROLINA BIOLOGICAL SUPPLY/PHOTOTAKE.

DO NOT MIX

Never mix parasite-control products without first consulting your vet. Some products can become toxic when combined with others and can cause fatal consequences.

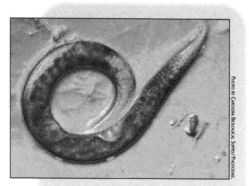

The roundworm *Rhabditis* can infect both dogs and humans.

ROUNDWORMS

Average-size dogs can pass 1,360,000 roundworm eggs every day. For example, if there were only 1 million dogs in the world, the world would be saturated with thousands of tons of dog feces. These feces would contain around 15,000,000,000 roundworm eggs.

Up to 31% of home yards and children's sand boxes in the US contain roundworm eggs.

Flushing a dog's feces down the toilet is not a safe practice because the usual sewage treatments do not destroy roundworm eggs.

Infected puppies start shedding roundworm eggs at three weeks of age. They can be infected by their mother's milk.

The roundworm, *Ascaris lumbricoides.*

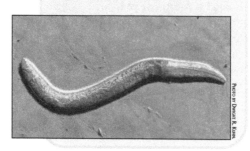

ROUNDWORMS

The roundworms that infect dogs are known scientifically as *Toxocara canis*. They live in the dog's intestines and shed eggs continually. It has been estimated that a dog produces about 6 or more ounces of feces every day. Each ounce of feces averages hundreds of thousands of roundworm eggs. There are no known areas in which dogs roam that do not contain roundworm eggs. The greatest danger of roundworms is that they infect people, too! It is wise to have your dog tested regularly for roundworms.

In young puppies, roundworms cause bloated bellies, diarrhea, coughing and vomiting, and are transmitted from the dam (through blood or milk). Affected puppies will not appear as animated as normal puppies. The worms appear spaghetti-like, measuring as long as 6 inches. Adult dogs can acquire roundworms through coprophagia (eating contaminated feces) or by killing rodents that carry roundworms.

Roundworm infection can kill puppies and cause severe problems in adults, as the hatched larvae travel to the lungs and trachea through the bloodstream. Cleanliness is the best preventative for roundworms. Always pick up after your dog and dispose of feces in appropriate receptacles.

The hookworm, *Ancylostoma caninum*.

HOOKWORMS

In the United States, dog owners have to be concerned about four different species of hookworm, the most common and most serious of which is *Ancylostoma caninum,* which prefers warm climates. The others are *Ancylostoma braziliense, Ancylostoma tubaeforme* and *Uncinaria stenocephala,* the latter of which is a concern to dogs living in the Northern US and Canada, as this species prefers cold climates. Hookworms are dangerous to humans as well as to dogs and cats, and can be the cause of severe anemia due to iron deficiency. The worm uses its teeth to attach itself to the dog's intestines and changes the site of its attachment about six times per day. Each time the worm repositions itself, the dog loses blood and can become anemic. *Ancylostoma caninum* is the most likely of the four species to cause anemia in the dog.

Symptoms of hookworm infection include dark stools, weight loss, general weakness, pale coloration and anemia, as well as possible skin problems. Fortunately, hookworms are easily purged from affected dog with a number of medications that have proven effective. Discuss these with your vet. Most heartworm preventatives include a hookworm insecticide as well.

Owners also must be aware that hookworms can infect humans, who can acquire the larvae through exposure to contaminated feces. Since the worms cannot complete their life cycle on a human, the worms simply infest the skin and cause irritation. This condition is known as cutaneous larva migrans syndrome. As a preventative, use disposable gloves or a "poop-scoop" to pick up your dog's droppings and prevent your dog (or neighborhood cats) from defecating in children's play areas.

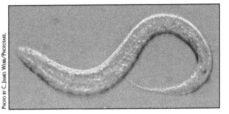

PHOTO BY C. JAMES WEBB/PHOTOTAKE.

The infective stage of the hookworm larva.

TAPEWORMS

Humans, rats, squirrels, foxes, coyotes, wolves and domestic dogs are all susceptible to tapeworm infection. Except in humans, tapeworms are usually not a fatal infection. Infected individuals can harbor 1000 parasitic worms.

Tapeworms, like some other types of worm, are hermaphroditic, meaning male and female in the same worm.

If dogs eat infected rats or mice, or anything else infected with tapeworm, they get the tapeworm disease. One month after attaching to a dog's intestine, the worm starts shedding eggs. These eggs are infective immediately. Infective eggs can live for a few months without a host animal.

The head and rostellum (the round prominence on the scolex) of a tapeworm, which infects dogs and humans.

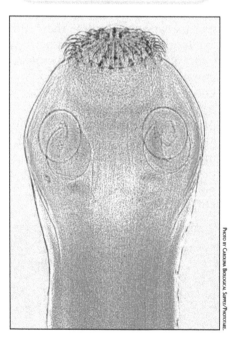

PHOTO BY CAROLINA BIOLOGICAL SUPPLY/PHOTOTAKE.

TAPEWORMS

There are many species of tapeworm, all of which are carried by fleas! The most common tapeworm affecting dogs is known as *Dipylidium caninum*. The dog eats the flea and starts the tapeworm cycle. Humans can also be infected with tapeworms—so don't eat fleas! Fleas are so small that your dog could pass them onto your hands, your plate or your food and thus make it possible for you to ingest a flea that is carrying tapeworm eggs.

While tapeworm infection is not life-threatening in dogs (smart parasite!), it can be the cause of a very serious liver disease for humans. About 50% of the humans infected with *Echinococcus multilocularis*, a type of tapeworm that causes alveolar hydatid, perish.

WHIPWORMS

In North America, whipworms are counted among the most common parasitic worms in dogs. The whipworm's scientific name is *Trichuris vulpis*. These worms attach themselves in the lower parts of the intestine, where they feed. Affected dogs may only experience upset tummies, colic and diarrhea. These worms, however, can live for months or years in the dog, beginning their larval stage in the small intestine, spending their adult stage in the large intestine and finally passing infective eggs through the dog's feces. The only way to detect whipworms is through a fecal examination, though this is not always foolproof. Treatment for whipworms is tricky, due to the worms' unusual life-cycle pattern, and very often dogs are reinfected due to exposure to infective eggs on the ground. The whipworm eggs can survive in the environment for as long as five years; thus, cleaning up droppings in your own backyard as well as in public places is absolutely essential for sanitation purposes and the health of your dog and others.

THREADWORMS

Though less common than round-worms, hookworms and those previously mentioned, thread-worms concern dog owners in the Southwestern US and Gulf Coast area where the climate is hot and humid. Living in the small intestine of the dog, this worm measures a mere 2 millimeters and is round in shape. Like that of the whipworm, the threadworm's life cycle is very complex and the eggs and larvae are passed through the feces. A deadly disease in humans, *Strongyloides* readily infects people, and the handling of feces is the most common means of transmission. Threadworms are most often seen in young puppies; bloody diarrhea and pneumonia are symptoms. Sick puppies must be isolated and treated immediately; vets recommend a follow-up treatment one month later.

HEARTWORM PREVENTATIVES

There are many heartworm preventatives on the market, many of which are sold at your veterinarian's office. These products can be given daily or monthly, depending on the manufacturer's instructions. All of these preventatives contain chemical insecticides directed at killing heartworms, which leads to some controversy among dog owners. In effect, heartworm preventatives are necessary evils, though you should determine how necessary based on your pet's lifestyle. There is no doubt that heartworm is a dreadful disease that threatens the lives of dogs. However, the likelihood of your dog's being bitten by an infected mosquito is slim in most places, and a mosquito-repellent (or an herbal remedy such as Wormwood or Black Walnut) is much safer for your dog and will not compromise his immune system (the way heartworm preventatives will). Should you decide to use the traditional preventative "medications," you can consider giving the pill every other or third month. Since the toxins in the pill will kill the heartworms at all stages of development, the pill would be effective in killing larvae, nymphs or adults, and it takes four months for the larvae to reach the adult stage. Thus, there is no rationale to poisoning the dog's system on a monthly basis. Lastly, do not give the pill during the winter months, since there are no mosquitoes around to pass on their infection, unless you live in a tropical environment.

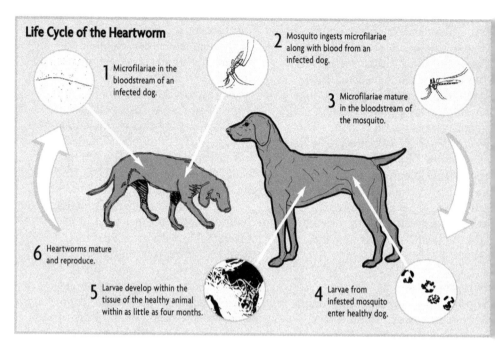

Life Cycle of the Heartworm

1 Microfilariae in the bloodstream of an infected dog.

2 Mosquito ingests microfilariae along with blood from an infected dog.

3 Microfilariae mature in the bloodstream of the mosquito.

4 Larvae from infested mosquito enter healthy dog.

5 Larvae develop within the tissue of the healthy animal within as little as four months.

6 Heartworms mature and reproduce.

HEARTWORMS

Heartworms are thin, extended worms up to 12 inches long, which live in a dog's heart and the major blood vessels surrounding it. Dogs may have up to 200 worms. Symptoms may be loss of energy, loss of appetite, coughing, the development of a pot belly and anemia.

Heartworms are transmitted by mosquitoes. The mosquito drinks the blood of an infected dog and takes in larvae with the blood. The larvae, called microfilariae, develop within the body of the mosquito and are passed on to the next dog bitten after the larvae mature. It takes two to three weeks for the larvae to develop to the infective stage within the body of the mosquito. Dogs are usually treated at about six weeks of age and maintained on a prophylactic dose given monthly.

Blood testing for heartworms is not necessarily indicative of how seriously your dog is infected. Although this is a dangerous disease, it is not easy for a dog to be infected. Discuss the various preventatives with your vet, as there are many different types now available. Together you can decide on a safe course of prevention for your dog.

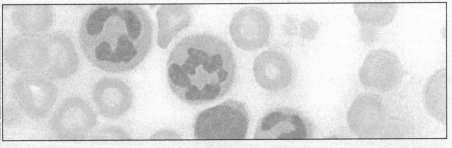

Magnified heart-worm larvae, *Dirofilaria immitis.*

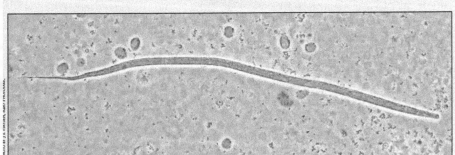

Heartworm, *Dirofilaria immitis.*

The heart of a dog infected with canine heart-worm, *Dirofilaria immitis.*

SHOWING YOUR
HAVANESE

INITIAL CONSIDERATIONS

If you want your Havanese to compete in dog shows, here are a few things you should know. First, your Havanese must know how to trot in a straight line, on leash, at his owner's left side. He must be able to stop on command and remain quiet while the judge does a physical examination that includes the mouth and, in the case of a male, the testicles. At all times, the dog should maintain the correct posture: head and neck held high and an alert disposition, whether moving or standing still.

Since small breeds are examined on a table, it is useful for you to teach your pup how to pose on an elevated surface, by holding up his head with your left hand and

Ambar, Champion of Champions, owned by Barbara Monteagudo and shared by Merita Batista and Zoila Portuondo, is showing off his ribbons. What could make a loving Havanese owner more happy than having her dog selected by the judge?

his tail with your right hand. Give him a command such as "Stay" and try to maintain this position for a few seconds and, in time, for two or three minutes. Every time he obeys you, caress him, praise him, let him know he's doing just what you asked him to do. For that reason, your dog must not identify the table with a disagreeable experience, such as having his nails cut (no dog enjoys having his nails trimmed), so find some place else to perform these tasks. Otherwise, he may resist when you try to pose him on the table for practice or during the show.

To train your dog to gait correctly, you must first make sure that his collar is placed high on the neck just behind the ears so he won't lower his head. If you use a choke collar, make sure the slip is always on top so you can control your Havanese from the other end of the leash, relaxing or applying the pressure of the collar on the dog's neck. Round leather check collars are generally used for training and a different type of collar, made of fine cord, is used in the show ring. Do not use a chain link collar on a Havanese as it can damage the dog's silky coat.

The correct way to pose a dog is as follows: maintain the head high, holding it with the collar or the left hand. The front legs should be perpendicular to the ground (or the table), solidly planted and parallel to each other. To do this, first hold one and then the other front leg at the elbow, raising each and lowering it into the proper position. The hindquarters are placed so the tarsal joints are completely perpendicular to the ground. This is accomplished by standing behind the dog while holding the leash with the left hand and raising first one and then the other rear paw to tarsus level. With your free hand, hold the tail up high.

Training sessions for shows should be given daily for 10 to 15 minutes twice a day. Don't let your dog become bored, since he should present a happy disposition at show time and not look as if he's performing a tedious duty. My advice is to give him five minutes of freedom before and after each session, so he can run happily around the yard and learn that a training session can also be fun.

Finally, before taking your Havanese to a show, attend one as a spectator. There you will watch experienced handlers and trained dogs at work. Ask questions; learn from them. Before you train your dog, you need to be trained to know exactly what to do and how to do it. You should know how to move in the ring, what steps to take so your Havanese trots properly, how to place him on the table, how to pose him, etc.

LIFE AS A SHOW DOG

There's still more to keep in mind if you plan to show your dog. A show dog has to be protected and cared for all the time. You can't allow him to go digging in the yard, rooting around the plants in the park or playing with puppies, because all of this can damage his coat. By this I don't mean you should make your dog a prisoner, as some handlers do. That would be abusive and harmful to his physical and temperamental health. However, it's obvious that you have to take different precautions with a show dog than you take with a family pet.

During the time you plan to present your dog in shows, try to have a professional groomer take care of his coat. The show dog

The judge will examine the Havanese's bite to be certain it is the desirable scissors bite.

The Havanese should act confidently and calmly as the judge makes the physical examination. This dog show is underway in Havana.

should also be perfectly socialized, since he has to share the ring with other dogs that he can neither attack nor fear. To ensure such behavior, he should be exposed to other dogs in his training, of course only once his vaccinations are complete.

It is also good for him to have enough exercise so he's in top shape physically and, therefore, won't pant or tire easily. This will naturally have a positive influence on the way your Havanese walks and trots in the ring.

Accustom your show dog to spend two or three hours at a time inside his crate, because that's where he will have to wait for his turn to enter the ring at the dog show. For show dogs, it's even more important that crate training is successful.

At the Europasieger Show, Sandra's Fantastic Mr. Florence, owned by Enka Fassott, has placed first in the group.

Remember that, before going to the show grounds, your Havanese must be bathed and carefully combed (don't divide the hair with the comb). Once you've found your

waiting place on the show grounds, comb and brush him by hand for the final touch before he enters the ring. Always take a bottle of water and coat conditioner with you so you can dampen the coat slightly to make it even more beautiful.

While awaiting your turn, keep your dog quiet inside his crate. Never permit him to run around the grounds. It is better to take advantage of whatever time you have to brush his coat and check him over to make sure your Havanese is impeccable when he meets the judge.

UNDERSTANDING THE DOG SHOW

To the uninitiated, showing a dog at a show may look easy, but you will learn very quickly that winning at a prestigious all-breed show takes many years of commitment, experience and hard work. The first concept that the canine novice learns when watching a dog show

is that each dog first competes against members of his own breed. Once the judge has selected the best member of each breed (Best of Breed), provided that the show is judged on a Group system, that chosen dog will compete with other dogs in his group. Finally, the dogs chosen first in each group will compete for Best in Show.

The second concept that you must understand is that the dogs are not actually compared against one another. The judge compares each dog against his breed standard, the written description of the ideal specimen that is approved by the hosting kennel club, such as the AKC or FCI. While some early breed standards were indeed based on specific dogs that were famous or popular, many dedicated enthusiasts say that a perfect specimen, as described in the standard, has never walked into a show ring, has never been bred and, to the woe of dog breeders around the globe, does not exist. Breeders attempt to get as close to this ideal as possible with every litter, but theoretically the "perfect" dog is so elusive that it is impossible.

Many hours of practicing your Havanese's heeling and gaiting will be rewarded when your dog moves like a pro around the ring.

If you are interested in exploring the world of dog showing, your best bet is to join your local breed club or the national parent club, which is the Havanese Club of America. These clubs often host both regional and national specialties, shows only for Havanese, which can include conformation as well as obedience and agility trials. Even if you have no intention of competing with your Havanese, a specialty is like a festival for lovers of the breed who congregate to share their favorite topic: the Havanese! Clubs also send out newsletters, and some organize training days and seminars in order that people may learn more about their chosen breed. To locate the breed club closest to you, contact the American Kennel Club, which furnishes the rules and regulations for all of these events plus general dog registration and other basic requirements of dog ownership.

The American Kennel Club offers three kinds of conformation shows: an all-breed show (for all

The judge carefully considers which dog most closely conforms to the ideal Havanese.

A judge in Havana examining the Havanese on the table. As with other Toy breeds, the handler must place the dog on the table for the judge to examine the dog's structure.

AKC-recognized breeds), a specialty show (for one breed only, usually sponsored by the parent club) and a Group show (for all breeds in the group). For a dog to become an AKC champion of record, the dog must accumulate 15 points at the shows from at least three different judges, including two "majors." A "major" is defined as a three-, four- or five-point win, and the number of points per win is determined by the number of dogs entered in the show on that day. Depending on the breed, the number of points that are awarded varies.

Dogs and bitches never compete against each other in the classes. Non-champion dogs are called "class dogs" because they compete in one of five classes. Dogs are entered in a particular class depending on their age and previous show wins. To begin, there is the Puppy Class (for 6- to 9-month-olds and for 9- to 12-month-olds); this class is followed by the Novice Class (for dogs that have not won any first prizes except in the Puppy Class or three first prizes in the Novice Class and have not accumulated any points toward their champion title); the Bred-by-Exhibitor Class (for dogs handled by their breeders or by one of the breeder's immediate family); the American-bred Class (for dogs bred in the US); and the Open Class (for any dog that is not a champion).

The judge at the show begins judging the Puppy Class, first dogs and then bitches, and proceeds through the classes. The judge places his winners first through fourth in each class. In the Winners Class, the first-place winners of each class compete with one another to determine Winners Dog and Winners Bitch. The judge also places a Reserve Winners Dog and Reserve Winners Bitch, which could be awarded the points in the case of a disqualification. The Winners Dog and Winners Bitch, the two that are awarded the points for the breed, then compete with any champions of record entered in the show, which are usually called "specials." The judge reviews the Winners Dog, Winners Bitch and all of the champions to select his Best of Breed. The Best of Winners is selected between the Winners Dog and Winners Bitch. Were one of these two to be selected Best of Breed, he or she would automatically be named Best of Winners as well. Finally the judge selects his Best of Opposite Sex to the Best of Breed winner.

At a Group show or all-breed show, the Best of Breed winners from each breed then compete against one another for Group One through Group Four. The judge compares each Best of Breed to his breed standard, and the dog that most closely lives up to the ideal for his breed is selected as Group One. Finally, all seven group winners (from the Toy Group, Hound Group, etc.) compete for Best in Show.

To find out about dog shows in your area, you can subscribe to the American Kennel Club's monthly magazine, the *American Kennel Gazette* and the accompanying *Events Calendar.* You can also look in your local newspaper for advertisements for dog shows in your area or go on the Internet to the AKC's website, www.akc.org.

If your Havanese is six months of age or older and registered with the AKC, you can enter him in a dog show where the breed is offered classes. Provided that your Havanese does not have a disqualifying fault, he can compete. Only unaltered dogs can be entered in a dog show, so if you have spayed or neutered your Havanese, your dog cannot compete in conformation shows. Altered dogs, however, can participate in other AKC events such as obedience trials and the Canine Good Citizen program.

Before you actually step into the ring, you would be well advised to sit back and observe the judge's ring procedure. It is best to stand back and study how the exhibitor in front of you is performing. The judge asks each handler to "stack" the dog, hopefully showing the dog off to his best advantage. The judge will observe the dog from a distance and from different angles, and approach the dog to check his teeth, overall structure, alertness and muscle tone, as well as consider how well the dog "conforms" to the standard. Also important, the judge will have the exhibitor move the dog around the ring in some pattern that he should specify (another advantage to not going first, but always listen since some judges change their directions—-and the judge is always right!). Finally, the judge will give the dog one last look before moving on to the next exhibitor.

If you are not in the top four in your class at your first show, do not be discouraged. Be patient and consistent, and you may eventually find yourself in a winning line-up. Remember that the winners were once in your shoes and have devoted many hours and much money to earn the placement. If you find that your dog is losing every time and never getting a nod, it may be time to consider a different dog sport or to just enjoy your Havanese as a pet. Parent clubs offer other events, such as agility, obedience, instinct tests and more, which may be of interest to the owner of a well-trained Havanese.

INDEX

Birth Date _____

Origin (Breeder's Name) _____

Breeder's Address _____ Phone _____

Registration/ID Number _____

Distinguishing Features _____

IN CASE OF LOST DOG

Vet's Name _____

Vet's Address _____ Phone _____

VACCINATION RECORD					
VACCINE	DATES				

CPSIA information can be obtained
at www.ICGtesting.com
Printed in the USA
LVHW06s2114210618
581304LV00003B/8/P

9 781621 871057